The Best of *Bead&Button*

Beadwoven Jewelry

Compiled by Lesley Weiss

Printed in the United States of America

06 07 08 09 10 11 12 13 14 10 9 8 7 6 5 4 3 2

ISBN-10: 0-87116-229-6
ISBN-13: 978-0-87116-229-8

Publisher's Cataloging-In-Publication Data
(Prepared by The Donohue Group, Inc.)

Beadwoven jewelry / compiled by Lesley Weiss.

   p. : ill. ; cm.
   Best of Bead&Button magazine
   ISBN: 0-87116-229-6

1. Beadwork--Handbooks, manuals, etc. 2. Beadwork--Patterns. 3. Jewelry
making. I. Weiss, Lesley. II. Title: Best of Bead&Button magazine. III. Title: Bead & Button.

TT860 .B43 2006
745.594/2

Senior art director: Lisa Bergman
Book layout: Sabine Beaupré
Photographers: Bill Zuback and Jim Forbes
Project editors: Julia Gerlach and Lesley Weiss

Acknowledgments: Tea Benduhn, Mindy Brooks, Terri Field, Lora Groszkiewicz, Kellie Jaeger, Carrie Jebe, Diane Jolie, Patti Keipe, Alice Korach, Pat Lantier, Tonya Limberg, Debbie Nishihara, Cheryl Phelan, Carole Ross, Salena Safranski, Candice St. Jacques, Maureen Schimmel, Kristin Schneidler, Lisa Schroeder, Terri Torbeck, Elizabeth Weber

CONTENTS

Introduction   4
Basics   5
Gallery   9

NETTING
Huichol bracelet   12
Ukrainian netted necklace   14
Netted pendant   17
Cabochon connection bracelet   20

HERRINGBONE
Subtle stripes band   24
Fiery blooms necklace   26
Rock garden bracelet   28
Rainforest band   32

PEYOTE
Dynamic cuff   36
Floating rings necklace   40
Autumn leaves brooch   43
Circuitry collar   46

BRICK
Diamond and arch bracelet   50
Starlight, star bright earrings   53
Cones of many colors   56
Gold-brick bracelet   58
Woven geometrics   61

LOOMWORK
Loomwork basics   66
Paisley choker   67
Layered loomwork pendant   70
Twisted bands   72

MORE STITCHES
A tapestry of beads   76
Criss-cross embellished bracelet   78
Dresden plate bracelet   80
Folded and gathered pendant   82
Fringe frenzy   84
Fuchsia trellis bracelet   86
Noughts and crosses bracelet   89
Extravagant earrings   92

Contributors   95
Index   96

INTRODUCTION

Beads offer unlimited versatility. Woven into a fabric or stitched into wonderfully complex strands, beads have become the material of choice for many jewelry designers because they can make intricate patterns and eye-catching textures using simple, inexpensive materials. A few beads and thread are all you need to start making beautiful, multi-dimensional jewelry.

Bead&Button readers and contributors have long known about the magic of beads and beadweaving. In *The Best of* Bead&Button *Magazine: Beadwoven Jewelry*, you'll find wonderful projects that demonstrate the talent and expertise of a great community of experts. The selection that follows includes more than 25 of the best on- and off-loom beadweaving projects ever published by the magazine. You'll be sure to wear the results with pride.

The fundamental stitches—netting, herringbone, brick, and peyote—are explained with photographs and illustrations to clarify the path the threaded needle takes through the beads at every step. The selected projects demonstrate beadweaving techniques clearly enough to be understood by beaders of all skill levels. The section on loomwork, for example, clearly explains the process for beginners, yet includes designs sure to intrigue experienced weavers. We've included an assortment of projects that use other common stitches—square stitch or right-angle weave among them—along with free-form stitches and combinations to demonstrate the possibilities.

If you are new to beadweaving, take time to explore the Basics section that begins on the next page. Familiarize yourself with the techniques and stitches included there before you begin. More advanced beaders, who can use the Basics section as a quick reference, can jump ahead to start enjoying the diversity of projects and approaches that follow. Feel free to adapt the designs to your own preferences. However you use this book, get started knowing that a relaxing and fun pastime awaits you with beadweaving.

Butterfly necklace by Erin Simonetti

BASICS

CONDITIONING THREAD

Conditioning straightens and strengthens your thread and also helps it resist fraying and tangling. Pull unwaxed nylon threads like Nymo through either beeswax (not candle wax or paraffin) or Thread Heaven to condition. Beeswax adds tackiness that is useful if you want your beadwork to fit tightly. Thread Heaven adds a static charge that causes the thread to repel itself, so it can't be used with doubled thread. All nylon threads stretch, so maintain tension on the thread as you condition it.

KNOTS

Working with beading cords and threads like Nymo, Silamide, or Fireline often requires knots for security.

half-hitch knot

Come out a bead and form a loop perpendicular to the thread between beads. Bring the needle under the thread away from the loop. Then go back over the thread and through the loop. Pull gently so the knot doesn't tighten prematurely.

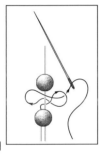

lark's head knot

Fold a cord in half and lay it behind a ring, loop, bar, etc. with the fold pointing down. Bring the ends through the ring from back to front, then through the fold. Tighten.

overhand knot

Make a loop and pass the working end through it. Pull the ends to tighten the knot.

square knot

1 Cross the left-hand cord over the right-hand cord, and then bring it under the right-hand cord from back to front. Pull it up in front so both ends are facing upward.

2 Cross right over left, forming a loop, and go through the loop, again from back to front. Pull the ends to tighten the knot.

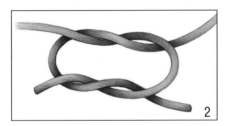

surgeon's knot

Cross the right end over the left and go through the loop. Go through again. Pull the ends to tighten. Cross the left end over the right and go through once. Pull the ends to tighten.

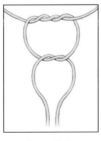

STOP BEAD

Use a stop bead to secure beads temporarily when you begin stitching. String the stop bead about 6 in. (15cm) from the end of your thread and go back through it in the same direction. If desired, go through it one more time for added security.

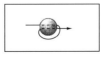

ADDING AND ENDING THREAD

Use one of these two methods to add and end thread.

1 Join the new thread to the old with a surgeon's knot and work it into the beadwork. After completing a row or two, weave the thread tails into the beadwork.

2 Start a new thread by tying it between beads a few rows before the point where you need to continue beading. Weave the new thread to that point, tying two or three half-hitch knots between beads. After working a row or two, finish off the old thread by weaving it into the new beadwork, tying two or three half-hitch knots between beads.

OPENING AND CLOSING LOOPS AND JUMP RINGS

Because wire gets brittle if it's worked too much, handle it as little as possible.

1 Hold the loop or jump ring with two pairs of chainnose pliers or chainnose and roundnose pliers, as shown.

2 To open the loop or jump ring, bring the tips of one pair of pliers toward you and push the tips of the other pair away.

3 String beads, loops, or other components onto the open jump ring. Reverse the steps to close the open loop or jump ring.

WIRE LOOPS

Wire loops are necessary any time you need to connect wire elements together. If you're new to working with wire, get some inexpensive craft or copper wire for your first attempts at making loops.

wrapped loop

1 Make sure you have at least 1¼ in. (3.2cm) of wire above the bead. With the tip of your chainnose pliers, grasp the wire directly above the bead. Bend the wire (above the pliers) into a right angle.
2 Using roundnose pliers, position the jaws in the bend.

3 Bring the wire over the top jaw of the roundnose pliers.
4 Reposition the pliers' lower jaw snugly into the loop. Curve the wire downward around the bottom of the roundnose pliers. This is the first half of a wrapped loop.

5 Position the chainnose pliers' jaws across the loop.
6 Wrap the wire around the wire stem, covering the stem between the loop and the top of the bead. Trim the excess wire and press the cut end close to the wraps with chainnose pliers.

CRIMPING

Crimping, usually used to secure flexible beading wire to a clasp, is the process of flattening or folding a crimp bead securely on your stringing material. Flattened crimps require only a pair of chainnose pliers, while folded crimps require a pair of crimping pliers.

flattened crimp

1 Hold the crimp bead using the tip of your chainnose pliers. Squeeze the pliers to flatten the crimp. Tug the clasp to make sure the crimp has a solid grip on the wire. If the wire slides, remove the crimp bead and repeat the steps with a new crimp bead.
2 Test that the flattened crimp is secure.

folded crimp

1 Position the crimp bead in the notch closest to the crimping pliers' handle.
2 Separate the wires and firmly squeeze the crimp.

3 Move the crimp into the notch at the pliers' tip and hold the crimp as shown. Squeeze the crimp bead, folding it in half at the indentation.
4 Test that the folded crimp is secure.

LADDER STITCH

A ladder of seed or bugle beads is most often used to begin brick stitch or herringbone. Pick up two beads, leaving a 4-in. (10cm) tail. Go through both beads again in the same direction. Pull the top bead down so the beads are side by side. The thread exits the bottom of the second bead (**a–b**). Pick up a third bead and go back through the second bead from top to bottom. Come back up the third bead (**b–c**).

String a fourth bead. Go through the third bead from bottom to top and the fourth bead from top to bottom (**c–d**). Continue adding beads until you reach the desired length.

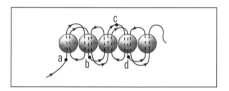

BRICK STITCH

1 Begin each row so no thread shows on the edge: String two beads. Go under the thread between the second and third beads on the ladder from back to front. Pull tight. Go up the second bead added, then down the first. Come back up the second bead.
2 For the remaining stitches on each row, pick up one bead. Pass the needle under the next loop on the row below from back to front. Go back up the new bead.

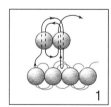
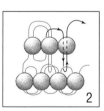

EVEN-COUNT FLAT PEYOTE

1 String a stop bead (remove the extra loop and weave the tail into the work after a few rows). String beads to total an even number. In peyote stitch, rows

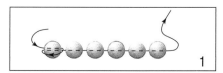

are nestled together and counted diagonally, so these beads actually become the first two rows.

2 To begin row 3 (the numbers in the drawings below indicate rows), pick up a bead and stitch through the second bead from the end. Pick up a bead and go through the fourth bead from the end. Continue in this manner. End by going through the first bead strung.

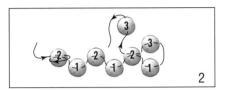

3 To start row 4 and all other rows, pick up a bead and go through the last bead added on the previous row.

EVEN-COUNT, CIRCULAR PEYOTE

1 String an even number of beads to equal the desired circumference. Tie in a circle, leaving some ease. Put the ring over a form if desired.
2 Go through the first bead to the left of the knot. Pick up a bead (#1 of row 3), skip a bead and go through the next bead. (Numbers in drawing indicate rows.) Repeat around until you're back to the start.

 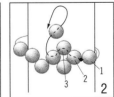

3 Since you started with an even number of beads, you need to work a "step up" to be in position for the next row.
Go through the first beads on rows

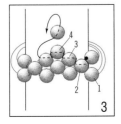

2 and 3. Pick up a bead and go through the second bead of row 3; continue in the same manner.

ODD-COUNT CIRCULAR PEYOTE

Follow steps 1 and 2 of even-count circular peyote above, but begin with an odd number of beads. Because you started with an odd count, you won't have to step up to the next row; you'll keep spiraling.

TWO-DROP PEYOTE STITCH

Work two-drop peyote stitch just like peyote stitch, but treat every pair of beads as if it were a single bead.
1 Start with an even number of beads divisible by four. Pick up two beads, skip the first two beads, and go through the next two beads. Repeat across, ending by going through the last two beads.

2 Pick up two beads and go through the last two beads added. Repeat across the row. To end, go through the first two beads, added on the previous row. Continue adding rows to reach the desired length.

RIGHT ANGLE WEAVE

1 To start the first row, string four beads and tie into a snug circle. Pass the needle through the first 3 beads again.
2 Pick up three beads (#5, 6, and 7) and sew back through the last bead of the previous circle and #5 and 6.

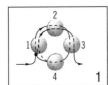 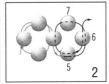

3 Pick up three beads and sew back through #6 and the first two new beads. Continue adding three beads for each stitch until the first row is the desired length. You are sewing circles in a figure-8 pattern and alternating direction with each stitch.
4 To begin row 2, sew through the last three beads of the last stitch on row 1, exiting the bead at the edge of one long side.

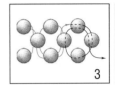

5 Pick up three beads and sew back through the bead you exited in step 4 (the first "top" bead of row 1) and the first new bead, sewing in a clockwise direction.

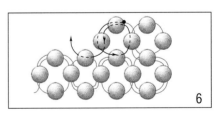

6 Pick up two beads and sew through the next top bead of the row below and the last bead of the previous stitch. Continue through the two new beads and the next top bead of the row below, sewing counterclockwise.

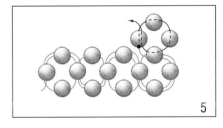

7 Sewing clockwise, pick up two beads, go through the side bead of the previous stitch, the top bead on the row below that you exited in step 5, and the first new bead. Keep the thread moving in a figure-8. Pick up two beads for the rest of the row. Don't sew straight lines between stitches.

SQUARE STITCH

1 String the required number of beads for the first row. Then string the first bead of the second row and go through the last bead of the first row and the first bead of the second row in the same direction. The new bead sits on top of the old bead and the holes are horizontal.

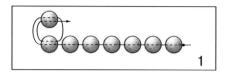

2 String the second bead of row 2 and go through the next-to-last bead of row 1 Continue through the new bead of row 2. Repeat this step for the entire row.

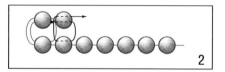

DECREASING SQUARE STITCH

To decrease the number of beads in the next row of square stitch, back-track through the next-to-last row, coming out the bead below where the new row will start. Go through the bead immediately above on the last row. Now begin the new row.

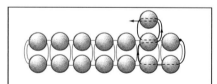

FLAT HERRINGBONE

Start with an even number of beads stitched into a ladder. Turn the ladder, if necessary, so your thread exits the end bead pointing up.

1 Pick up two beads and go down through the next bead on the ladder (**a–b**). Come up through the third bead on the ladder, pick up two beads, and go down through the fourth bead (**b–c**). Repeat across the ladder.

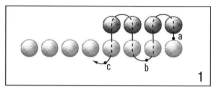

2 To turn, come back up through the second-to-last bead and continue through the last bead added in the previous row (**a–b**). Pick up two beads, go down through the next bead in that row, and come up through the next bead (**b–c**). Repeat across the row.

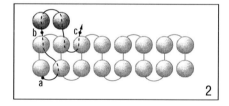

NDEBELE, TUBULAR

To work tubular Ndebele, make a ladder of the desired even number of beads (in this case four) and join it into a ring. String two beads and go down the next bead on the row below (the ladder). Come up the next bead and repeat. There will be two stitches when you've gone down the fourth bead (**a–b**).

You need to work a "step up" to be in position to start the next row. To do this, come up the bead next to the one your needle is exiting and the first bead of the first stitch (**b–c**). Continue adding two beads per stitch and stepping up at the end of each round.

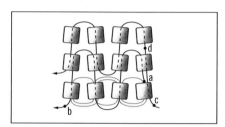

GALLERY

Fringe and brick stitch necklace by Lisa Olson Tune

Netted motif necklace by Marilyn K. Lowe

Loomwork cuffs by Ellen Friedenberg

Peyote stitch box by Judy Walker

Flower necklace by Kathy Travis

*Black and white bracelets by
Christine Marie Noguere*

NETTING

Huichol bracelet

The Huichol Indians of Mexico have developed a distinctive style of beadweaving that produces intricate, symmetrical designs through a two-needle netting technique. While many netting Huichol designs are stitched with tiny size 15º beads, this simpler version is worked in size 11º beads.

by **Sylvia Sur**

The bracelet's stitched portion is 6½ in. (16cm) long with 12 design repeats. Add or remove complete design units to change the size. To substitute 15º beads for the 11ºs, use finer thread and stitch more repeats to increase the length.

Netted band

When you work with two needles, it's easier to have the working needle on the right-hand side when you start each row, so you can work the row from right to left (reverse for lefties).

[1] Thread a needle with 6 yd. (5.5m) of conditioned Nymo (Basics, p. 5). Wind half the thread onto a bobbin until the netting is established. Each step below begins with the beads you pick up to add to the pattern.

Row 1, right-hand (first) needle (**figure 1, a–b**):
Two As and a B five times, then four As. Slide the beads against the bobbin.

Row 2, first needle (**b–c**):
a. Two Bs, then go through the last B on the previous row.
b. Three Bs, go through the next B. Repeat three more times.
c. Two Bs and slide them against the other beads. Undo the bobbin and thread the second needle on the tail.

Row 3, second needle (**a–d**):
a. Two As, through the last B.
b. Two Bs, C, through the next B.
c. C, D, C, through B.

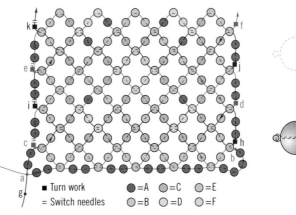

d. C, E, C, through B.

e. C, D, C, through B.

f. C, two Bs, through last B on row 2.

Row 4, second needle (**d–e**):

a. Two As, two Bs, through B.

b. C, two Ds, through D.

c. C, two Es, through E

d. Two Es, C, through D.

e. Two Ds, C, through B.

f. Two Bs. Slide the beads against the netting.

Row 5, first needle (**c–f**):

a. Two As, through B.

b. Two Bs, C, through D.

c. A, two Es, through E.

d. C, F, C, through E.

e. Two Es, A, through D.

f. C, two Bs, through B.

Row 6, first needle (**f–g**):

a. Two As, two Bs through B.

b. C, two Es, through E.

c. C, two Fs, through F.

d. Two Fs, C, through E.

e. Two Es, C, through B.

f. Two Bs.

Row 7, second needle (**e–h**):

a. Two As, through B.

b. Two Bs, C, through E.

c. Two Es, C, through F.

d. Three Fs, through F.

e. C, two Es, through E.

f. C, two Bs, through B.

Row 8, second needle (**h–i**):

a. Two As, two Bs, through B.

b. C, D, A, through E.

c. Two Es, C, through F.

d. C, two Es, through E.

e. A, D, C, through B.

f. Two Bs.

■ = Turn work   ● =A   ◐ =C   ◑ =E

= = Switch needles   ○ =B   ○ =D   ○ =F

FIGURE 1

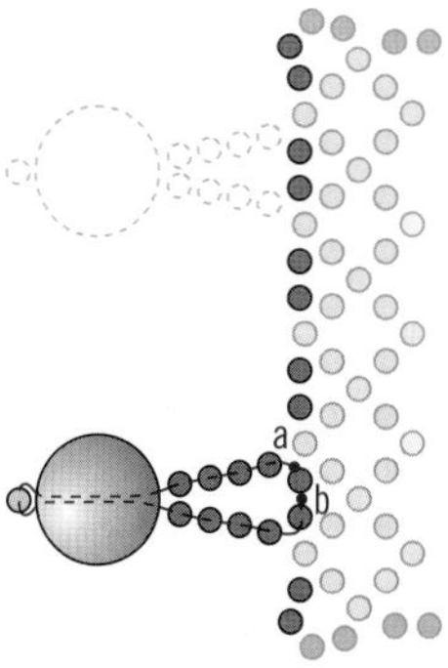

FIGURE 3

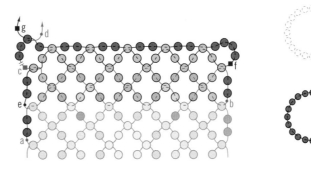

FIGURE 2

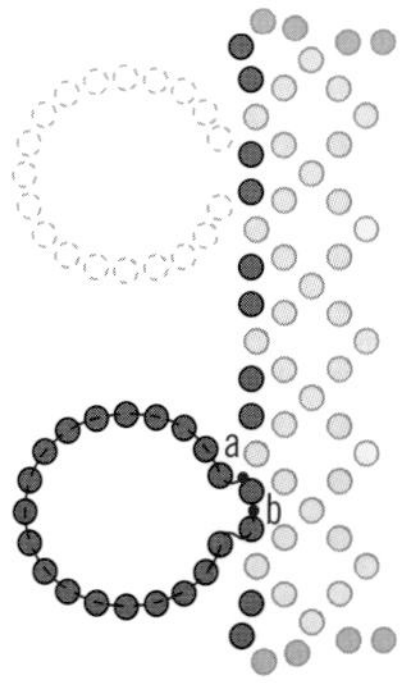

FIGURE 4

Row 9, first needle (**g–j**):

a. Two As, through B.

b. Two Bs, C, through D.

c. Two Ds, A, through E.

d. Three Es, through E.

e. A, two Ds, through D.

f. C, two Bs, through B.

[2] Repeat rows 4–9 until you are one design unit from the desired length. As you stitch row 4 in the body of the bracelet, substitute A (black) beads for C (metallic purple) beads in steps c and d. Then, at the last repeat, omit row 9 and work the following rows to finish the border.

Row 1, first needle (**figure 2, a–b**):

a. Two As, through B.

b. Two Bs, C, through D.

c. Two Ds, C, through E.

d. Three Es, through E.

e. C, two Ds, through D.

f. C, two Bs, through B.

Row 2, first needle (**b–c**):

a. Two As, two Bs, through B.

b. C, B, C, through D.

c. C, B, C, through E.

d. C, B, C, through D.

e. C, B, C, through B.

f. Two Bs.

Row 3, second needle (**d–e**):

a. Two As, through end B.

b. Three Bs, through B.

Repeat four times.

c. Three Bs, through B.

Row 4, second needle (**e–f**):

a. Four As, through B.

b. Two As, through B. Repeat four times.

c. Two As and slide to netting.

d. (**c–g**) Two As through the end A.

Clasp

[1] Start with at least 18 in. (45cm) of thread. Exit through an A on the short edge (**figure 3, point a**).

[2] String four As, an 8mm bead, and a 2mm bead. Go back through the 8mm bead, string four As, and go through the second A of the base pair (**a–b**). Go through the beads again to reinforce them.

[3] Skip two pairs of As and repeat step 2. Secure the thread with a few half-hitch knots (Basics) and trim.

[4] Anchor a new thread at the other end and exit an A as in step 1 (**figure 4, point a**). String 19 As (or enough to go over the 8mm bead) and go through the second A of the base pair (**a–b**). Go through the loop again.

[5] Skip two pairs of As and make a second loop as in step 3. Secure the thread in the netting with half-hitch knots and trim. ●

MATERIALS

bracelet 7½ in. (19cm)

• 5g each of size 11º Japanese seed beads:
    opaque black, color A
    violet-lined purple, color B
    metallic purple, color C
    turquoise, color D
    metallic matte gray, color E
    AB rosy red, color F

• 2 8mm beads

• 2 2mm beads or size 11º seed beads

• Nymo D

• beeswax or Thread Heaven

• beading needles, #12

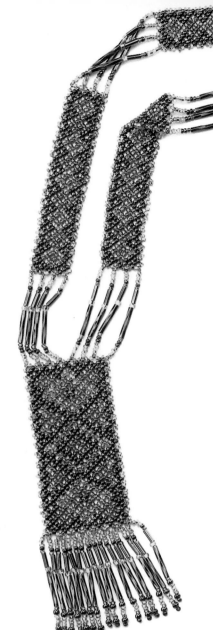

Ukrainian netted necklace

Join woven panels with beaded strands

by **Maria M. Rypan**

Netting is a very forgiving technique where irregular beads can get worked into the fabric without showing. However, you need to cull the beads to make sure that the accent and connector beads are consistent in size. You must sort the bugles to select the straightest, most even ones of equal length.

The kilim-patterned medallion, two midsection bands, and one long back band are worked individually in horizontal netting, following the charted patterns. If you use size 11º seed beads instead of 10ºs, add extra motifs to the back band to achieve the desired length. Next, join the netted pieces with strands of connector beads and finish with a double fringe.

Netting basics
• This three-bead netting has one bead on each side of each connector bead throughout. Color changes create the design motifs, and color sequences change each row.
• Read and work each chart

horizontally from the bottom up. The first row forms the lower edge, and you'll use the bottom connector beads for hanging the fringe or to connect the bands.
• Tighten the thread as you work. Tight tension allows you to see the connector beads on the previous row.
• Two gold beads outline each side edge. The right-hand edge forms automatically as you bead, but you'll have to add the gold beads on the left-hand edge after completing the strip.

Medallion
[1] String a stop bead (Basics, p. 5) 9 in. (23cm) from the end of a 60-in. (1.5m) length of beading thread. You'll remove this bead to complete row 2.

MATERIALS
necklace
• size 10º seed beads (size 11º seed beads can be substituted):
  1 hank each:
  silver-lined gold, color A
  blue iris, color B
  ½ hank each:
  silver-lined light brown, color C
  silver-lined blue, color D
• **32** blue iris 15mm bugle beads
• **32** blue iris #3 bugles
• **32** blue iris size 8º seed beads
• **32** silver-lined gold size 8º seed beads
• beading needles, #10 or #12
• Nymo B beading thread
• beeswax or Thread Heaven

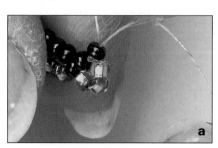

a

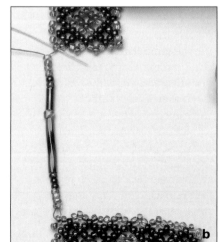

b

[2] Pick up beads #1–34 (**figure 1**).

[3] To start row 2, go back through the edge point bead (#29) toward the start. Pick up three Bs for the next stitch (#35–37) and go through the next B on the row below (#25). Continue adding three beads per stitch. End the row by picking up one B (#53) and going through the first B on the row below (**figure 2**).

[4] Remove the stop bead, and tighten both threads. Tie a surgeon's knot to keep the foundation rows tight (Basics and **photo a**).

[5] Pick up three Bs and go through the center bead on the stitch below. The piece may twist until you've added a few rows, so be careful to go through the correct beads (**figure 3**, p. 16).

[6] Follow the medallion chart to complete the piece, using a marker to keep track of the color changes, and tighten the work as you go.

[7] On the top (A) row, connect the last A to the middle B on the left-hand side (**figure 4, a–b**). Then string two As and go through the next middle edge bead (**b–c**). Repeat for **c–d**. Keep the work tight and continually square up the medallion.

[8] Every so often, secure the thread by circling through an adjacent mesh unit next to the newly added edge beads (**d–e**). Check to make sure the piece remains square.

[9] Continue edging through the start bead and bottom edge beads #2–3. This is where you'll start the fringe. You can work it now or as the last step. If a long thread remains, leave it for the fringe. If the thread is short, end it in the beadwork.

Midsections and back band

Both midsections and the back band use the same chart, a small two-rhomb pattern repeated as many times as necessary to achieve the desired length. Work these pieces with the same netting technique as the medallion.

[1] Start as in **figure 5**. The repeat pattern is eight rows, as marked on the chart. Work 4½ repeats for the two midsections and 19½ repeats for the back band. You may need more repeats for the back if you use size 11º beads.

[2] Bead from the start through row 10, then work the repeat as many times as necessary. Finish with the half-repeat marked on the chart and the top two rows. Then add the edge beads along the left-hand side as for the medallion.

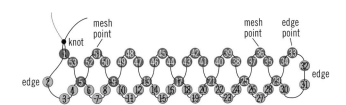

edge points = 1, 29
mesh points = 5, 9, 13, 17, 21, 25
fringe points = 3, 7, 11, 15, 19, 23, 27, 31

FIGURE 1

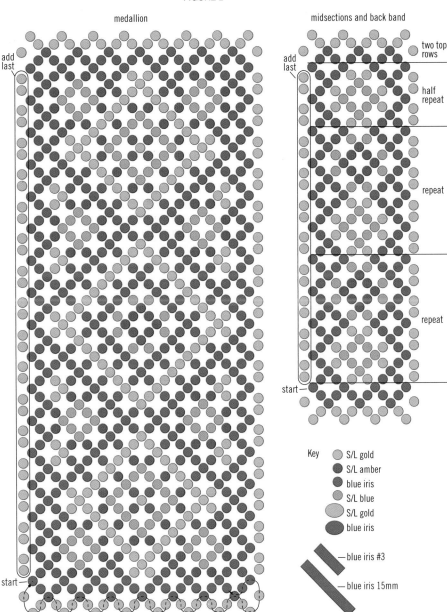

FIGURE 2

medallion

midsections and back band

two top rows

half repeat

repeat

repeat

Key
- S/L gold
- S/L amber
- blue iris
- S/L blue
- S/L gold
- blue iris

— blue iris #3

— blue iris 15mm

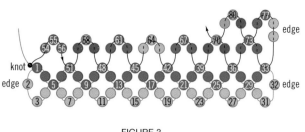

FIGURE 3

FIGURE 4

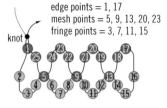

edge points = 1, 17
mesh points = 5, 9, 13, 20, 23
fringe points = 3, 7, 11, 15

FIGURE 5

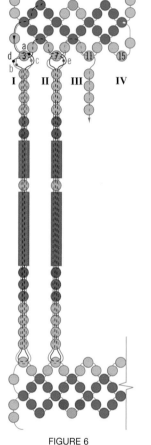

FIGURE 6

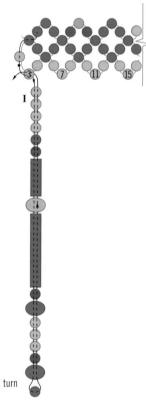

FIGURE 7

FIGURE 8

Connector joinings

When the four netted pieces are finished, join them by stringing a sequence of beads between the connector points.

[1] Secure a 60-in. (1.5m) length of thread in a midsection, and emerge from the center bead on the first bottom stitch.

[2] Pick up the sequence of connector beads shown in **figure 6**.

[3] Go through the matching top-edge connector bead on the medallion and then sew back up the connector sequence (**a–b**). Go through the midsection connector bead from the opposite direction (**b–c** and **photo b**).

[4] Retrace the thread path (**c–d**), zigzag through the netting to the next connector bead.

[5] Repeat steps 2 and 3 to make the next connector (**d–e**).

[6] Retrace the thread path and repeat steps 2–5 to make the additional connectors.

[7] After making the four connectors between a midsection and one side of the medallion, sew back through the connector thread path to the beginning for security and to tighten and square up the necklace.

[8] Connect the other midsection to the other side of the medallion as in steps 1–4.

[9] Make sure the back section is not twisted, and connect the ends to the tops of the midsections as in steps 1–4.

Fringe

Do not pull the fringe tight. Work loosely so it will fall gracefully.

[1] If you left a long thread at the bottom of the medallion, start fringing with it. Otherwise, secure a 60-in. (1.5m) thread in the medallion, emerging left to right from bead #3.

[2] String the fringe sequence as shown in **figure 7**. Skip the last seed bead, and sew back up the fringe. Go through the same fringe point in the opposite direction.

[3] String a second fringe from the same fringe point. Go back up the

fringe, through the fringe point from left to right, and follow the netted edge to the next fringe point. The two fringes should straddle the fringe point (**figure 8**).

[4] Repeat steps 2 and 3 across the bottom of the medallion. ●

Netted pendant

Catch a cabochon in a beaded web

by **Maria Ahasgina**

If you want to incorporate stone slices or cabochons in your beadwork, try this simple beadweaving technique to create a harmonious ensemble. The technique works best with thin cabochons because the woven bezel is narrow.

To some extent, the size of the cabochon determines the size of the beads used to weave the strip that holds it. The large agate (above) is encased with 8º seed beads, the medum-size fossil with 11º seeds, and the small agate with 15º seeds.

Weave around the cabochon

[1] Thread a needle with 1 yd. (.9m) of conditioned Nymo (Basics, p. 5). Leaving a 3–4 in. (8–10cm) tail, string one color A seed bead. Go through it again in the same direction (the extra thread pass will be removed before joining the ends of the base row).

[2] Pick up four As, three Bs, and four As. Go through the stop bead in the opposite direction (**figure 1, a–b**, p. 19, and **photo a**, p. 18).

[3] Pick up three Bs and four As, and go through bead #9 (**b–c** and **photo b**).

a

b

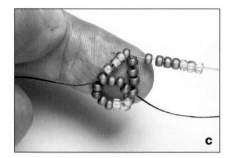

c

d

e

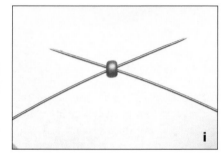

f

g

h

i

j

k

[4] Pick up three Bs and four As. Go through bead #16 (**c–d** and **photo c**).
[5] Repeat steps 3 and 4 as many times as needed to go around the cab.
[6] Wrap the woven strip around the cab, leaving a space large enough to accommodate an upper and lower set of three Bs (**photo d**).
[7] Pick up three Bs and sew through bead #5 (**figure 2, a–b** and **photo e**).
[8] Pick up three As and sew through the A at the end of the woven piece (**b–c** and **photo f**).
[9] Use the tip of your needle to remove the extra thread pass from the first bead strung. String three Bs and sew through bead #1 (**c–d**). Pull tight

and tie the tail and working thread with a surgeon's knot (Basics).

Weave the front row
[1] Using 1 yd. of conditioned Nymo, start a new thread. Exit the middle bead of any three-B group (**photo g**).
[2] Pick up one A and sew through the middle bead of the next group of three Bs (**figure 3, a–b**).
[3] Repeat step 2 around the front edge. Sew through the middle B in the first set again and pull tight.

Weave the back rows
[1] Keeping the tension tight, weave to the back of the cab.

MATERIALS
necklace
- 3 x 5cm cabochon or stone
- size 8º seed beads:
  8g color A
  3g color B
- 2 split rings
- S-hook clasp or 1½-in. (3.8cm) 16-gauge wire
- beading needles, #10 or #12
- Nymo to match bead color
- beeswax or Thread Heaven
- G-S Hypo Cement
- roundnose pliers
- wire cutters

[2] Exit the middle bead of any B set. Pick up three Bs and go through the middle bead of the next B group. Repeat around the back edge. Sew through the middle B in the first set again and pull tight.
[3] Pick up two Bs and repeat step 2, but pick up two Bs each time. End the thread securely. The photo on p. 19 shows the completed back.

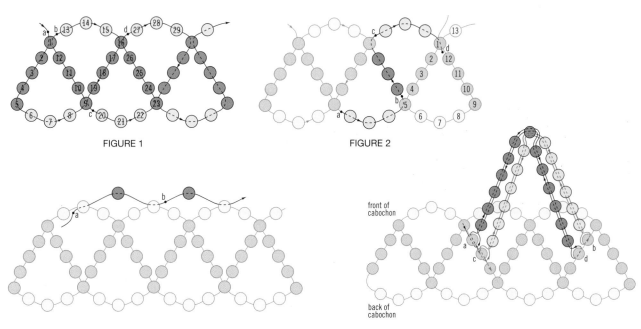

FIGURE 1

FIGURE 2

FIGURE 3

FIGURE 4

front of
cabochon

back of
cabochon

Make the bail
Turn the beadwoven cab into a
pendant by adding a beaded bail.
[1] Start a new thread and weave
over to bead a (figure 4) at the top
of the cab. Sew through a, pick up
13 As, and sew through d. Go back
through the beads just strung and
pull tight.
[2] Go through c, pick up six As, and
go through the seventh bead of the
loops made in the previous step.
[3] Pick up six As and go through b.
Retrace the thread path back to c. Tie
off the thread. Photo h shows the
completed bail.

Make the chain
Weave the chain in two parts. First,
form the base row with a simple
two-needle stitch. Then embellish it
with a three-bead stitch that spirals
around the chain. Alternatively, use
single-needle right-angle weave (Basics)
for the base chain.
[1] Start with a 3-yd. (2.7m) length of
conditioned Nymo. Thread a needle
onto each end and pull 1 yd. through
each needle.
[2] Pick up one split ring and one A
and slide them to the center of the
thread. Pass one needle through both
several times.

[3] Pick up one A with each needle
and snug them next to the first A.
[4] Pick up one A and pass both
needles through it in opposite
directions (photo i). Snug this bead
against the last beads strung (photo j).
[5] Repeat steps 3 and 4 for the
desired length of the chain. End
with step 4.
[6] Pick up the other split ring and
pass both needles through it and the
last A several times. Secure the tails.
[7] Thread a needle with 1 yd. of
Nymo and begin at either end of the
chain. Go through bead a (figure 5).
[8] Pick up one A, a B, and an A. Sew
down through b. Turn the chain over.
[9] Pick up one A, a B, and an A.
Sew down through c. Turn.
[10] Repeat steps 8 and 9 along
the chain.

Add the finishing touches
[1] Carefully slide the chain through
the loops of the bail.
[2] Slide an S-hook onto a split ring
at one end of the chain. Use pliers to
press this end of the hook closed so it
will not come off.
[3] To make an optional handmade
embellished S-hook, use pliers to bend
a 1½-in. (3.8cm) piece of 16-gauge
wire into an S shape. Wrap 24-gauge

front of
chain

back of
chain

FIGURE 5

wire around the hook
several times. Slide on an A
and wrap the wire around
the hook one or two times.
Slide on another bead and
wrap. Repeat around the
hook as desired (photo
k). End by wrapping
wire around the
other end of the
hook. Fasten the
S-hook to a
split ring as
described in
step 2. ◗

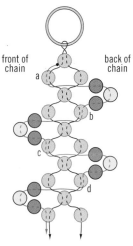

Cabochon connection bracelet

Make a striking bracelet by stitching together several bezeled cabochons. The beaded bezel consists of netting combined with square stitch.

Change the bezel pattern by reversing the color sequence of the seed beads on every other cab. Sew the cabs together, accent with bugles and seeds, and attach the clasp with heart-shaped beads.

Bezel the cabochons

All the cabs in this bracelet are 20mm rounds, mainly for the ease of explaining the technique. Once you bead around one, however, you'll be able to adjust the pattern for any cab size. Just make sure you start with enough beads in step 1 to cover the front of the cab so it won't fall out. Then adjust the number of netted rows to fit the size of the cab (steps 3–6).

[1] Start with a 1½-yd. (1.4m) length of thread and string a repeating pattern of two color A and one color B seed beads for a total of 39 beads. Sew through the beads again in the same direction to form a ring. Tie the threads together with a surgeon's knot (Basics, p. 5).
[2] Go through the first two As and one B on the ring (**figure 1, a–b**).
[3] Pick up an A, a B, and an A. Sew through the next B on the ring (**b–c**). Repeat around the ring (**c-d**). Step up

FIGURE 1

FIGURE 2

Make a bracelet of netted cabochons

by **Yulia Crystal**

by sewing through the first B on the ring and the first A and B on the second row (**d–e**).

[**4**] Repeat step 3 to add another row.

[**5**] Pick up three As and go through the next B (**figure 2, a–b**). Repeat around the ring (**b–c**) and step up through the first two As (**c–d**). This row will fold under the previous row, becoming the first row on the back of the cabochon.

[**6**] Place the cabochon in the beadwork so the front of the cab is

centered in the bead ring from step 1. Pick up two As and go through the middle A of the next three-bead set on the previous row (**figure 3, a–b**). Repeat around the ring and step up through the first A (**figure 4, a–b**).

[**7**] Pick up an A and square stitch it to the bead the thread exits (**b–c**). Sew through the next three As on the previous row (**c–d**). Repeat around the row.

[**8**] Your thread should exit the bead under the first A square-stitched on

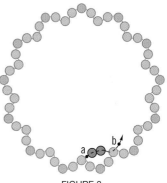

FIGURE 3

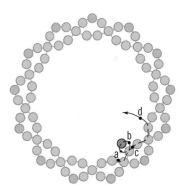

FIGURE 4

a

b

the row (**figure 5, point a**). Working clockwise, sew through the first A, pick up an A, and sew through the next (**a–b**). Repeat around the row.

[9] Sew through the circle of beads again to tighten them, and secure the circle with a few half-hitch knots (Basics) between beads.

[10] Weave through to a B on the edge row (step 4). Pick up an A, a B, and an A and sew through the next B (**photo a**). Repeat around the cab to add a ruffle to the outside edge. Secure the thread and tail in the beadwork, and trim.

[11] Repeat steps 1–10 with the remaining cabs, alternating the color sequence as desired.

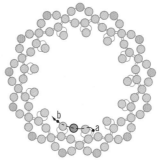

FIGURE 5

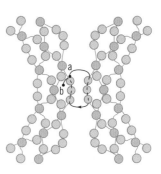

FIGURE 6

Assemble the bracelet

[1] Place the cabs in a row in the order they will be sewn together. Start a new thread and secure it in the bezel of the first cab, leaving an 8-in. (20cm) tail. Position the needle so the thread exits an end bead of a three-bead ruffle (**figure 6, point a**). Go through the adjacent three-bead set on the second cab, and go back through the three-bead set on the first (**a–b**). Go through the beads again in the same direction to reinforce the join.

[2] Pick up a bugle bead and sew through the three-bead set on the second cab (**figure 7, a–b**). Sew through the bugle and up through the three-bead set on the first cab (**b–c**). Go through the beads again to secure.

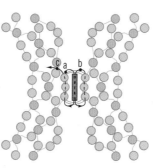

FIGURE 7

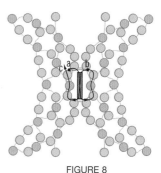

FIGURE 8

[3] Weave through the beadwork or end the thread and start a new one. Position the needle so it exits the second cab as in **figure 6, point a.** Connect the remaining cabs in the same way.

Occasionally, the three-bead sets may not line up perfectly. In this case, refer to **figure 8** and sew the cabs together between the ruffled edge beads.

[4] Position the needle so it exits on the outside edge of the last cab. Pick up a seed bead, a crystal, a heart bead, a crystal, and a seed bead. Go through the soldered jump ring and back through the beads just strung (**photo b**). Sew through the next three-

bead set on the edge, and weave the thread back through the beadwork so it exits at the same edge bead as before. Retrace the thread path a few more times and trim the thread.

[5] Thread a needle on the tail and repeat step 4 to attach the lobster claw as you did the jump ring. ●

HERRINGBONE

Subtle stripes band

Take an Ndebele herringbone bracelet from flat to fabulous
with a mix of matte and shiny triangle beads

by **Perie Brown**

This sophisticated bracelet covers all the angles. Glinting triangle beads give the surface a fabric-like texture when stitched into a herringbone band. Up the ante with the designer's touch of slanting stripes to create a bracelet with unbeatable appeal.

Herringbone band

[1] Assign each of the eight triangle bead colors a letter from A–H. Determine the finished length and subtract the length of your clasp. This will give you the length of the beaded band.

[2] Start a 2-yd. (1.8m) length of conditioned thread (Basics, p. 5). Leaving a 12-in. (30cm) tail, use the color pattern in **figure 1** to construct a ladder (Basics) with two beads per stack for 16 stacks.

[3] Work a row of flat Ndebele herringbone (Basics) off the ladder row, referring to the pattern (**figure 2, a–b**) for the color changes. At the end of the row, turn without adding an edge bead, as shown in **figure 2, b–c.**

[4] Continue working in herringbone, following the pattern, until you reach the desired length.

[5] Reinforce the last row with a second thread path but don't cut the thread.

Clasp

[1] With the working thread, sew through the first loop on the clasp and under the thread bridge between the first two beads in the last row (**figure 3, a–b**).

[2] Continue sewing through the loops on the clasp and the thread bridges until the clasp is secure. Retrace the thread path to reinforce the join.

[3] Repeat on the other end of the bracelet using the 12-in. tail. ❍

MATERIALS
bracelet 7½ in. (19cm)
- triangle beads, size 11º, 2.5g each of **8** colors
- 5-strand slide clasp
- Nymo D conditioned
- beeswax
- beading needles, #12

FIGURE 1

FIGURE 3

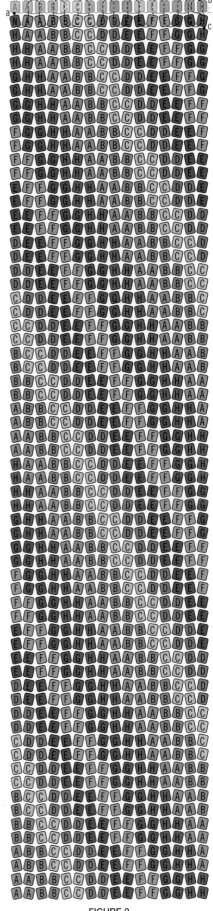

FIGURE 2

Fiery blooms necklace

A stunning floral bead ignites a crystal Ndebele herringbone rope

by **Debbie Nishihara**

Bicone crystals provide a marvelous setting for a gorgeous hibiscus bead. Adding a dramatic twist to the herringbone rope allows the crystals to nestle together.

Herringbone tubes

The number of crystals in the materials list makes two 7-in. (18cm) herringbone tubes for an overall necklace length of 18 in. (46cm). This necklace used approximately 32 crystals per inch (2.5cm), so if you want to lengthen or shorten the tubes, be sure to adjust the number of crystals as well.

[1] Using a comfortable length of beading cord, make a ladder (Basics, p. 5) following the color pattern shown in **figure 1, a–b**.

[2] Join the beads into a ring by coming up the first color A, down the last B, and back up the first A (**figure 2, a–b**). The bicone shape prevents this row from lining up as usual, so be sure to note which are the tops of the beads.

[3] Pick up an A and a B, and go down through the next B (**figure 3, a–b**). Come up the next A, pick up an A and a B, and go down the next B (**b–c**).

[4] To add a gentle spiral to the herringbone tube, modify the stitch slightly, as follows: Come up through both As in the next stack, pick up an A and a B, and go down through the first B in the next stack (**figure 4, a–b**). Come up through both As in the next stack, pick up an A and a B, and go down through the next B (**b–c**).

Repeat until the tube is 7 in. long. When you finish the tube, leave the needle on the working thread. Secure the beginning thread in the beadwork. Make a second herringbone tube.

Assembly

[1] Add 6 in. (15cm) to the combined measurement of your two tubes and cut a piece of flexible beading wire to that length. My beading wire is 20 in. (51cm) long.

[2] String a cone, a spacer, a rondelle, a spacer, and an accent bead (**photo a**). Then string a triangle, a crimp bead, a triangle, and a clasp half (**photo b**). Go back through all the beads and the cone, and crimp the crimp bead (Basics). With the clasp face-up, the end

a

b

c

d

e

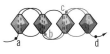

FIGURE 1

FIGURE 2

FIGURE 3

FIGURE 4

components should look like those in **photo c**.

[3] Hold the tube vertically, trimmed-end first, and drop the beading wire down into it in small increments (**photo d**). Slide the tube into the cone.

[4] Using the thread with the needle still attached, sew through several beads to close the tube around the beading wire. Make several half-hitch knots (Basics) and trim the tail.

[5] String the focal bead and the other herringbone tube (**photo e**). Close the other end of the tube around the beading wire as in step 4.

[6] Repeat step 2 to finish the other end of the necklace. Do not pull the wire too tightly before you crimp, or the herringbone tubes will buckle. ●

MATERIALS

necklace 18 in. (46cm)

- hibiscus bead (Alethia Donathan, DACS Beads, 808-842-7714, dacsbeads.com)
- 4mm Swarovski bicone crystals
  224 fire opal, color A
  224 green tourmaline AB, color B
- **2** 10mm marcasite cones
- **2** 8mm faceted citrine rondelles
- **2** 6mm silver accent beads
- **4** 5mm daisy-shaped silver spacers
- **4** size 5º triangles, lime with copper
- linked-leaves sterling toggle clasp (Candice Wakumoto, 808-625-2706, candicewakumoto@msn.com)
- DandyLine beading cord, .008
- flexible beading wire, .014–.015
- beading needles, #12
- **2** crimp beads
- crimping pliers
- wire cutters

Rock garden bracelet

Embellish a tubular herringbone band with bezeled cabochons

by **Leslee Frumin**

Bezeled cabochons and an embellished ruffle take this band from basic to brilliant. The ruffle is more than pure fancy—it disguises the clasps, integrating them into the design.

Weaving the band

Use beads in two shades of the same color—shiny and matte—for the top side of the band and a solid contrasting or neutral color for the lining or underside.
[1] Thread a comfortable length of beading thread on a needle. Then weave a ladder (Basics, p. 5, or use the shortcut explained in step 2) with 20 beads, alternating colors A and B for the first ten and color C for the second ten.
[2] The shortcut ladder method is as

follows: Pick up 20 beads as described in step 1 to 4–6 in. (10–15cm) from the end of the thread. Take the needle back through the next-to-last bead in the direction it was originally strung (**photo a**). Manipulate the beads so they are side-by-side. Go through the 18th bead in the direction it was strung and position it alongside the 19th bead (**photo b**). Repeat until you've gone through the first bead.
[3] Make sure the ladder isn't twisted and connect the end to the beginning by going through the bead at the opposite end, then back through the bead at the first end (**photo c**).
[4] With your needle exiting the first A bead, begin tubular herringbone stitch (Basics): Pick up a B and an A and go down the second bead on the

ladder (**photo d**). Then come up the third bead (**figure 1, a–b**, p. 31). Pick up a B and an A, go down the fourth bead (**photo e**, p. 30), and come up the fifth to begin the next stitch (**b–c**). Repeat until you've gone down the tenth bead.

Come up the first color C bead and make five stitches with Cs. To begin the second herringbone row, step up through the first bead on the row your needle is exiting (in this case, the ladder; in future, the row below the last row added), and continue up the first bead added on the row (**d–e** and **photo f**). Pick up an A and a B and continue working herringbone (**e–f**). The step-up is at **point g**. Continue stitching in herringbone, alternating As and Bs for each row until the

band is ¼ in. (6mm) shorter than the desired length.

[5] When you need to add thread, leave the needle with the old thread in place. Start the new thread several rows below the last stitch and tie two or three half-hitch knots (Basics) between beads as you weave the new needle along the thread path. When you exit the same bead as the needle with the old thread, continue with the new thread. After working a few rows, end the old thread the way you added the new thread.

Working the wave

Work the wave or ruffle with seven rows of flat herringbone (Basics) on the top color beads only. The idea is to increase the number of stacks,

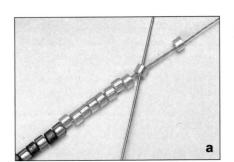

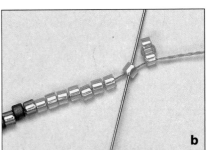

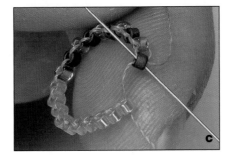

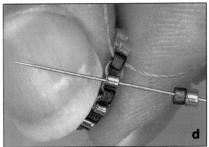

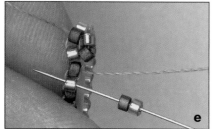

which creates the wave. Maintain the checkerboard color pattern. Pay attention to the position of the increases because they skew the position of the beads on the regular stitches. In all, you make three waves coming out of the last row on the band.

[1] Make the first wave as follows:

Row 1: Work a regular flat row of five herringbone stitches following the checkerboard pattern on the top side of the band. After you've added the fifth stack, your needle will be going down the end bead on the row below (**figure 2, point a**). Come up the bead next to the one the needle exits (**a–b**), then continue up the end bead on the last row (**b–c** and **photo g**).

Row 2: Work one stitch. With the needle in position to add the beads for the next stitch, pick up one A or B to

begin an increase (**figure 3, a–b**). Then go down the second bead on the row below and come up the next bead to work the next stitch (**b–c**). Work three stitches, add one more increase bead, and work the last stitch.

Row 3: Make one regular stitch (**d–e**), go through the single increase bead, pick up two beads (**e–f**), and go through the single bead again in the same direction (**f–g**). Come up the bead on the other side of the single bead (**g–h**) and make three regular stitches. Make another two-bead increase over the single bead increase. End with a regular stitch. The two beads of the increase will lie somewhat horizontally, although the tight space will tend to push them into the shape of a herringbone stitch.

Row 4: Work a regular stitch. Treat the two increase beads as a regular herringbone stitch—come up the first bead, pick up two beads, and go down the second bead (**i–j**). Work a regular stitch, add a bead, work a regular stitch, add a bead. Work three regular stitches.

Row 5: Work like row 3, putting two beads over the single bead increases and working the other stitches normally.

Row 6: Work like row 4, treating the two-bead increases like regular stitches, but do not add new increases.

Row 7: Work nine regular stitches.

[2] You can embellish the top of each herringbone stitch on the wave in one of three ways:

a. Exit the first bead of a stitch and pick up an accent bead and a size 14º bead. Go back down the accent bead and the second bead of the stitch as shown in **figure 4**.

b. Square stitch two beads onto the top of a herringbone stitch, and embellish as in option a (**figure 5**).

c. Square stitch a group of four beads onto the top of the herringbone stitch and embellish as in option a (**figure 6**).

[3] For the second wave, sew down to row 1 of the wave and position the needle so it comes out the top of an end bead on that row. Repeat rows 2–7 on the top side of the first wave and embellish the top.

[4] For the third wave, sew back down to row 1 of the original wave and position the needle so it exits the top of an edge bead on the other side of the first wave. Begin the third wave (**photo h**). Repeat rows 2–7 on the side opposite from the second wave and embellish the top.

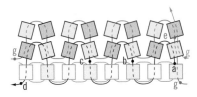

FIGURE 1

FIGURE 2

FIGURE 4

FIGURE 5

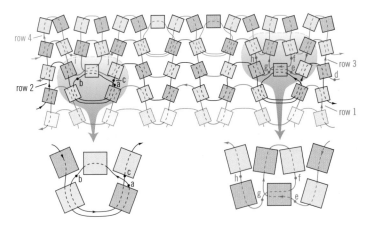

FIGURE 3

FIGURE 6

Bezeling cabochons

[1] Trace the cabochons on Ultrasuede, and cut out each piece slightly larger than the stone.

[2] Secure each stone to the suede with a piece of double-sided tape.

[3] Thread your needle with a comfortable length of conditioned thread (Basics), knot the end, and come up through the suede right next to the stone.

[4] Pick up three color A beads and sew back to the wrong side of the suede. Come up between the first and second beads, and go through the second and third beads again (figure 7). Repeat this step until the stone is encircled.

[5] Work peyote stitch (Basics) off the circle of beads for several rows toward the top of the cabochon (photo i). The number of rows depends on the thickness of the stone. Work the last two rows with size 14º seed beads so they hug the stone securely (photo j).

[6] Zigzag back down the side of the bezel to the base row and work a row of peyote stitch in the other direction to cover the Ultrasuede (photo k). Do not cut the tail.

[7] Bezel as many stones as desired.

Joining the parts

[1] Cut a strip of Ultrasuede the length and almost the width of the herringbone band. Attach a threaded needle to one end and pull it through the band. Be sure to keep the suede flat (photo l).

[2] With the slide clasp closed, stitch all three loops to the ladder end of the bracelet, going through them several times and catching the Ultrasuede in the stitches (photo m).

[3] Repeat step 2 to attach the clasp at the other end.

[4] Stitch the cabochons onto the band, sewing through the Ultrasuede on the bottom of the cabochon and through the top beadwork and the suede liner. Then sew through every few beads at the bottom of the bezel, attaching them to the beads on the cuff (photo n). If necessary, add cylinder beads between the bezel and the band to neaten the join. If you sew down through the liner beads, be careful not to pull so tightly that you dimple the beadwork. ●

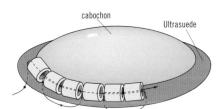

FIGURE 7

MATERIALS

bracelet 7 in. (18cm)

- Japanese cylinder beads:
  5g each of **2** colors, A and B
  10g lining color, C
- 2g seed beads, size 14º
- **27** assorted 3–4mm accent beads:
  pearls, semi-precious stones,
  sterling, etc.
- **3–6** 10–15mm stone or glass
  cabochons
- Silamide or Nymo D beading
  thread
- 3-loop slide clasp
- beeswax
- beading needles, #12-15
- 8-in. (20cm) square lightweight
  Ultrasuede
- double-sided tape or Terrifically
  Tacky Tape

Rainforest band

An exotic flower explodes with color on a gradated herringbone cuff

by **Carole Horn**

This spectacular bracelet captures the vibrant colors of the rainforest with several shades of green in both matte and shiny finishes and a spiky flower worked in a brilliant contrasting hue. The finished bracelet should measure about 1 in. (2.5cm) larger than your wrist. This bracelet is 7 in. (18cm).

Flowers

[1] Using a comfortable length of Fireline, pick up five color E beads and tie the tail and working thread together using a surgeon's knot (Basics, p. 5 and **figure 1**).
[2] Go through the bead next to the knot. Pick up one bead between each of the five beads in the circle (**figure 2, a–b**).
[3] Working in circular peyote (Basics), stitch a total of six rows, stepping up at the end of each row. Keep the tension tight as you stitch, so the beads form a small tube.
[4] Pick up nine Es and one C. Skip the C, and sew back through the last E (**figure 3, a–b**). Pick up seven Es and sew through the first of the nine Es and the up bead. Exit the next up bead (**b–c**). Snug up the beads to make them stand.
[5] Repeat until there are five petals.
[6] To create the spikes, hold the five petals up toward the center. Sew through the same up bead that started the first petal and pick up nine Es and one C (**figure 4, a–b**). Skip the C, sew back through the

nine Es, and go through the next up bead (**b–c**). Continue making spikes around the row.
[7] Drop down one row and make a spike in each bead. Repeat. It takes about 40 spikes and five center petals to make a full flower.

Herringbone band

For maximum contrast, start with the darkest green and work so the lightest green falls in the middle of the bracelet. The instructions for the specific color changes in this bracelet are given here, but you can easily design your own version. Once the first half is finished, simply repeat the colors and number of rows in reverse to mirror it. To introduce each new color, alternate one pair of new color beads with one pair of the old color for three rows before completely changing over to the new color.
[1] Start with a ladder of 16 two-bead stacks (Basics) using color D. Sew through the first, last, and first stack to join the ladder into a ring.
[2] Work in tubular herringbone (Basics and **figure 5**) through the top bead of each of the two-bead stacks for ten rounds. Step up to start each new round.
[3] To increase, pick up two Ds and sew down through the top bead of the next stack (**figure 6, a–b**). Pick up one C and sew up through the top bead of the next stack (**b–c**). Repeat around the tube.

[4] Pick up two Ds and sew down through the top bead of the next stack, as before (**figure 7, a–b**). Pick up two Cs and sew up through the top bead of the next stack (**b–c**). Repeat around the tube. You have now increased the bracelet band from 16 to 32 beads.
[5] Work two rounds of herringbone stitch, alternating two Ds and two Cs (**figure 8**).
[6] To stitch the gradient pattern in the bracelet shown below, work as follows:
Rounds 15-20: color C.
Rounds 21-23: alternate two Cs and two Bs.
Rounds 24-32: color B.
Rounds 33-36: alternate two Bs and two As.
[7] Continue in herringbone in A until the tube is about 2¼ in. (6cm) shorter than the desired length. Then work the gradient pattern in reverse (rounds 36–15), followed by two rounds that alternate two Cs and two Ds.
[8] The decreases at this end of the bracelet mirror the increases at the start. To begin, pick up two beads, sew down through the top bead of the next stack, and come up through the top bead of the following stack (**figure 9, a–b**). For the second stitch, pick up one bead, sew down through the top bead of the next stack, and come up through the top bead of the following stack (**b–c**). Repeat these

two stitches around the tube. Step up to start the next round.

[9] Pick up two beads and sew down through the top bead of the next stack (**figure 10, a–b**). Sew through the single bead at the top of the next stack and come up through the top bead of the following stack (**b–c**). Repeat to the end of the round and step up.

[10] Work one more row as in step 9, passing through the single bead to prevent it from sticking out of the beadwork (**figure 11, a–b**).

[11] Work in herringbone stitch over the 16 remaining beads for ten rows.

[12] Flatten the band and sew each end shut.

Peyote toggle

[1] Working in flat peyote (Basics), stitch a ten-bead band for ten rows, using Ds as at the start of the herringbone band.

[2] Roll the strip into a tube and zip up the ends (**photo a**). Flatten the tube for your closure (**photo b**).

[3] Anchor a new thread at one end of the bracelet. Exit at the middle near the edge row. Sew through two beads near the middle of the toggle and then sew back into the bracelet. Sew through a bead or two and repeat several times.

[4] To make the loop closure (**photo c**), anchor a thread and exit at either folded edge. Pick up 18 Ds (enough to go over your toggle) and sew into several beads at the opposite fold. Repeat to reinforce the loop.

Embellishment

[1] Anchor a thread near the toggle, exiting a few rows from the edge. Pick up four color F beads, sew through a bracelet bead, and go back through the last vine bead. Repeat, branching off to the left side.

[2] Pick up a leaf and three Fs. Go through the last F on either stalk.

[3] To make a bud, pick up three Es and go through the last F on the other stalk.

[4] Add beads and leaves as desired. Repeat on the other end of the bracelet, leaving room to add the large flower.

[5] Anchor a thread at the loop end. Sew into several beads at the base of the flower and back into the bracelet, positioning the flower close to the bracelet's edge. Repeat until the flower is securely attached. ❍

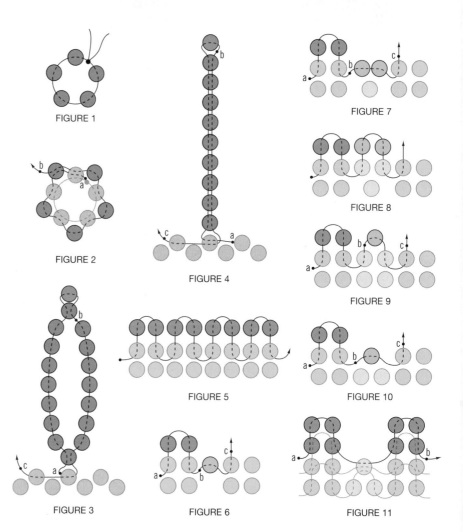

FIGURE 1

FIGURE 2

FIGURE 3

FIGURE 4

FIGURE 5

FIGURE 6

FIGURE 7

FIGURE 8

FIGURE 9

FIGURE 10

FIGURE 11

MATERIALS

bracelet 7 in. (18cm)

- size 11º seed beads
  20g, lime matte, color A
  15g, lime AB shiny, color B
  15g, dark green mix shiny, color C
  15g, forest green matte, color D
  15g, bright color for flower
  and buds, color E
  5g, earth color for vines, color F
- **7** pressed-glass leaves
- Fireline 6-lb. test
- beading needles, #12

PEYOTE

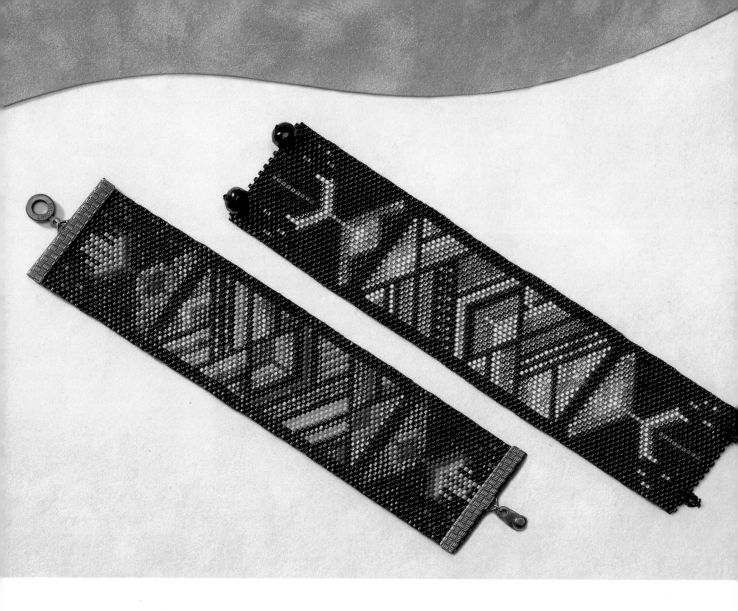

Dynamic cuff

Here's an easy way to work odd-count flat peyote

by **Sylvia Sur**

Odd-count flat peyote is sometimes avoided because the turn on one side is a bit tricky, and results in either a stiff or unstable edge, depending on the method used. But some designs, like this colorful cuff, require a center row, leaving no option but to use an odd-count stitch. This easy two-needle method does away with the tricky turn and produces beautiful results with identical edges.

Follow either chart 1 or chart 2 on p. 39. Begin at the left-hand corner of the main panel. When it's complete, set it aside without finishing off the tails. Beginning at the lower left-hand corner, make two side panels. Position one side panel at each end of the main panel, making sure they are mirror images of each other, and join them (Basics, p. 5) temporarily. Stitch additional rows if necessary for fit.

When the band is the right length, join the sections. Weave the tails into the beadwork with a few half-hitch knots between beads. Trim the excess.

Each pattern is charted with a specific clasp type in mind to produce a 7-in. (18cm) bracelet. The warm-color chart is meant to finish with end bars and a ball clasp, while the cool-color chart is designed to be finished with two 6mm beads and bead loops.

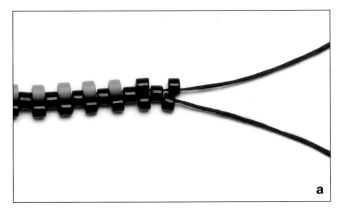

a

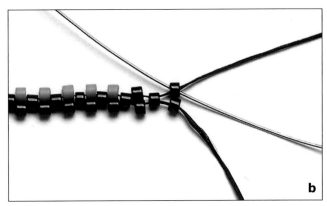

b

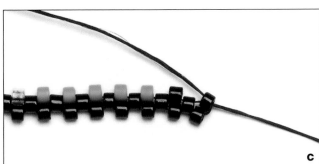

c

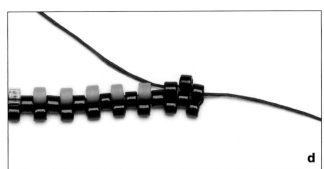

d

Keep this in mind and adapt the patterns appropriately if you decide to use a different type of clasp. If using the beads and loops, try making the loops with an elastic thread such as Gossamer Floss or Stretch Magic— they make buttoning the bracelet easier. If you wish to make the bracelet longer, stitch wider sections of black between the main and side panels and/or at the ends.

Two-thread odd-count peyote bracelet

To start the bracelet, work steps 1–3 below, or follow the directions for "Starting peyote with two needles" on p. 38.

[1] Thread a beading needle at each end of a 2-yd. (1.8m) length of beading thread and string a stop bead to the center (Basics, p. 5). Pick up 29 black cylinder beads with one needle and slide them against the stop bead.

[2] With the same needle, work row 3 in peyote stitch (Basics). This is the first row that uses colored beads. You'll pick up a total of 15 beads for this row, with the last one left loose for the moment. Put the first needle down.

[3] Remove the stop bead and pull both threads to restore the tension

to the first three rows. The first and the last beads are loose on the two threads at the same end of the piece (**photo a**).

[4] Pick up the needle exiting row 1 and go through the loose bead at the at the end of row 3 (**photo b**). You have made the turn. Pull on both threads. Notice that this bead has a thread going through it in each direction (**photo c**).

[5] Pick up the first bead of row 4, and go through the next up bead (**photo d**). Tighten by pulling both threads. Work row 4 and make the easy turn at the end.

[6] Using the same needle, work row 5. At the end of row 5, pick up the last bead, but do not stitch it. Let it sit loosely (**photo e**).

[7] Pick up the other needle, and go back through the last bead (**photo f**). Pull on both threads to adjust the tension, pick up one bead and go through the next up bead (**photo g**). Adjust the tension again, then complete the next row following the chart, make the easy turn, and work the next row.

[8] Repeat step 7 for the rest of the panel, following the color changes on the chart.

MATERIALS
bracelet 7 in. (17.5cm)
• Japanese cylinder beads, in the colors listed on the chart or your own choices:
  10g black DB10, 1—2g each of **14** warm colors or **12** cool colors
• Nymo B
• beading needles, #11–#12
• pair of end bars, copper, size 1, and ball and socket clasp (Diane H. Designs, 262- 574-1324 or dianehdesigns@ execpc.com) or 2 6mm rondelles

Adding thread

When you're down to about 4 in. (10cm) of thread on each needle, you need to add thread. Add new thread at the end of an odd-numbered row, even if one of the threads is long enough to keep working.

[1] At the end of an odd-numbered row, bury the short waiting thread that you would have used to make the turn by weaving it back into the work, tying a few half-hitch knots between beads (Basics). Trim.

[2] Thread 3 yd. (2.7m) or more of thread with a needle at each end. Go through the end bead where the waiting thread was toward the edge.

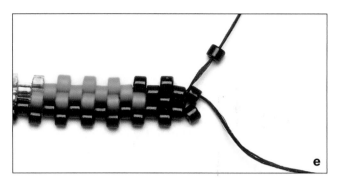

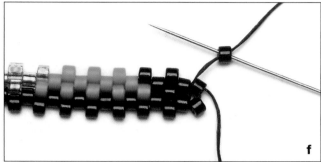

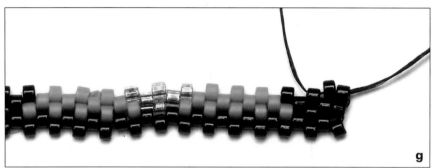

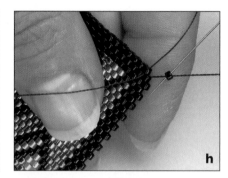

Starting peyote with two needles

This start, as popularized by Suzanne Cooper on her Web site—suzannecooper.com/classroom/twoneedle.html—is the ideal method for starting two-needle, odd-count flat peyote. It does away with the stop bead, and you put on the first three rows at once so you are ready to make the two-needle turn easily when you've finished stringing the width of the cuff.

[1] Center two beads on a 4-yd. (3.6m) length of beading thread with a needle on each end.
[2] Pick up one bead with the needle in your non-dominant hand. Using the needle in your dominant hand, go through the bead in the same direction (both needles exit the same side—photo j). Be careful not to split the thread. Then pull

both threads to tighten the bead against the first two strung.
[3] Pick up a bead on each needle and slide them to the middle (photo k).
[4] Repeat steps 2 and 3. Continue in this manner until you have the correct number of beads for the first three rows, ending with a step 3.
[5] Make the odd row turn as described in step 4 of "Two-needle odd-count flat peyote bracelet."

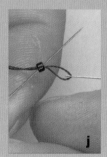

To use the loop closure, sew out of a bead near one end (two or three rows in, and about five beads from the edge). Pick up a rondelle and a black cylinder bead, and go back through the rondelle. Sew into the beadwork in the same place, go through a few beads, and exit from the same bead so you can retrace the thread path. Repeat on the other side with the other rondelle. Make loops at the opposite end of the bracelet, each with enough beads to fit around the rondelle. **o**

Pull half the thread through. The needle at the other end of this new thread is idle on the table.
[3] Make the turn with the new thread (photo h) and work the pattern for a few beads. Adjust the tension. At this point you have to pull on three threads to get the tension even.
[4] Bring the second needle on the new thread through the end bead

where the short thread exits (photo i). Then bury the short thread. The new thread is in position to work the next odd turn.

Finishing
To attach the bar end clasp, simply position each component over an end of the band and squeeze it closed with chainnose or flatnose pliers.

CHART 1   CHART 2

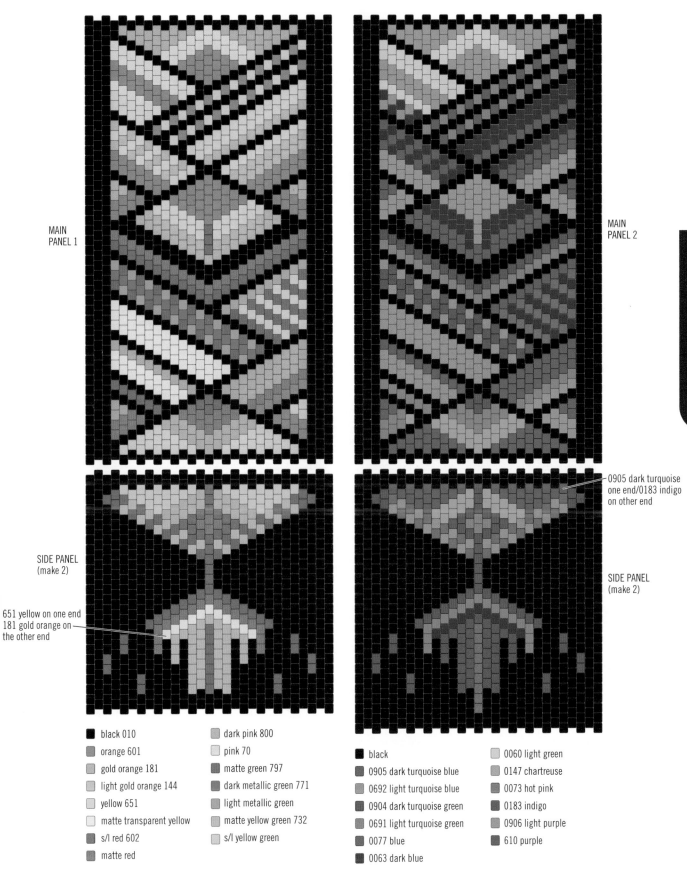

MAIN
PANEL 1

MAIN
PANEL 2

0905 dark turquoise
one end/0183 indigo
on other end

SIDE PANEL
(make 2)

SIDE PANEL
(make 2)

651 yellow on one end
181 gold orange on
the other end

- ■ black 010
- ■ orange 601
- ■ gold orange 181
- ■ light gold orange 144
- ■ yellow 651
- ■ matte transparent yellow
- ■ s/l red 602
- ■ matte red

- ■ dark pink 800
- ■ pink 70
- ■ matte green 797
- ■ dark metallic green 771
- ■ light metallic green
- ■ matte yellow green 732
- ■ s/l yellow green

- ■ black
- ■ 0905 dark turquoise blue
- ■ 0692 light turquoise blue
- ■ 0904 dark turquoise green
- ■ 0691 light turquoise green
- ■ 0077 blue
- ■ 0063 dark blue

- ■ 0060 light green
- ■ 0147 chartreuse
- ■ 0073 hot pink
- ■ 0183 indigo
- ■ 0906 light purple
- ■ 610 purple

Floating rings necklace

Showcase a cluster of sliding beaded beads on a peyote rope

by **Bonnie O'Donnell-Painter**

This necklace uses a single stitch in combination with multiple bead sizes and colors to create a piece of jewelry that is fun to make and wear. This design features a surprise—the beaded rings are captured in the center of the necklace, and they can spin and slide around.

Beaded beads

This necklace has seven beaded beads —three pairs and one centerpiece bead with a row of 3mm fire-polished beads in its center. Make as few as three or as many as nine beads, and feel free to make each different. If you want to add more than nine beads, make more rows in the center section of your rope so all the beads fit.

[1] Thread a needle with 1 yd. (.9m) of Nymo or Fireline. String eighteen 11° seed beads. Tie the beads into a circle with a surgeon's knot (Basics, p. 5), leaving a 5-in. (13cm) tail. There should be some ease between the beads.

[2] Sew through the bead next to the knot. Pick up an 11°, skip a bead, and go through the next bead (**photo a**). Continue working in even-count tubular peyote (Basics) for five rows, stepping up to begin each new row.

[3] Pick up three 15° seed beads and go through the next bead (**photo b**). Repeat around the outside of the peyote ring. When you add the last set of 15°s, bring the needle through the first 11° and the one diagonally below it to the left (**photo c**). Go through one more bead diagonally below so your needle exits a bead on the third row of the ring.

[4] Pick up a 15°, an 11°, and a 15° and go through the next bead in the row (**photo d**). Repeat around the center of the ring. After the last set, go through the 11° and diagonally through the 11°s below until the needle exits a bead on the other edge (**photo e**).

[5] Add three 15°s between every edge bead as in step 3 (**photo f**).

[6] End the thread by tying half-hitch knots (Basics) between a few beads. Trim the thread. Repeat with the tail.

[7] Repeat steps 1–6 to make a second bead to match the first.

[8] Make two more two-bead sets using different color combinations. Also try starting the embellishment on the second row of the ring, or add embellishment to each row. You can also vary the number of rows in each ring. For example, make a ring with three rows and on the last row stitch a tiny teardrop between each up bead. This is the fun part—experiment!

[9] For the center bead, make a ring with five rows and embellish the

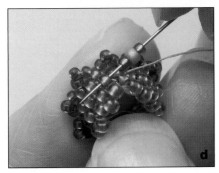

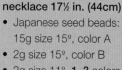

MATERIALS

necklace 17½ in. (44cm)

- Japanese seed beads:
  15g size 15º, color A
- 2g size 15º, color B
- 2g size 11º, **1–3** colors
- 3g size 8º
- 9 3mm fire-polished beads
  (optional)
- 9 tiny teardrops (optional)
- assorted accent beads: teardrops,
  3–4mm fire-polished beads, size 6º
  seed beads, etc.
- button
- Nymo B or Fireline fishing line,
  6-lb. test
- beading needles, #12

center row with a 15º, 3mm fire-polished bead, and a 15º between each bead. Add embellishment to the edges of the ring.

Peyote rope

[1] Thread a needle with a 2-yd. (1.8m) length of thread. Pick up eight size 15º color A seed beads. Tie the beads into a circle with a surgeon's knot, leaving an 8-in. (20cm) tail.
[2] Work in tubular peyote for a total of 40 rows.
[3] Use color B 15ºs for the next three rows. Use size 11º seed beads for three rows (**photo g**). Keeping the tension firm so the thread doesn't show, work two rows with size 8º seed beads (**photo h**).
[4] Work one row with your beads (**photo i**).
[5] Reverse the rows in step 3 so the last three rows are 15ºs.
[6] Repeat steps 2–5 twice more.
[7] Now you are at the middle section of the necklace. Stitch 95 rows of tubular peyote using color A 15ºs. If you are adding more beaded beads, you might need to add a few extra rows to this section so the beads can move freely.
[8] String the beaded beads on the peyote rope.
[9] Make the second half of the necklace to match the first. You will

have three accent bead sections on each side of the sliding rings.
[10] Go through the four up beads on the last row to close the end of the peyote tube.
[11] Pick up five 15ºs, the loop on the button, and five 15ºs, and go through a bead on the other side of the peyote rope (**photo j**). Retrace the thread path (**photo k**) a couple of times and secure the thread with half-hitch knots. Trim.
[12] Thread a needle on the tail at the other end, and repeat step 10. String enough 15ºs to make a loop that fits around the clasp component. Reinforce the loop with several thread passes, and end the thread. ●

Autumn leaves brooch

Wire enhances a sculptural peyote pin

by **Dottie Hoeschen**

Make these peyote leaves in a riot of fall colors, or choose a subdued palette of rich metallics. Either way, this leaf pin will be a fabulous addition to your fall wardrobe. Stitch the leaves separately, then attach them to a base, and embellish them with more beads and wire.

Once you master the leaves, experiment to see what else you can create with them. This brooch easily converts to a necklace by

adding it to a stitched neckband. Individual leaves also can be used to make a pair of playful earrings.

Small amounts of thread show along the edges as you taper the leaves. To minimize its appearance, choose a thread color that closely matches your cylinder beads.

Basic leaf shape
[1] Thread your needle with a yard (.9m) of Nymo or Fireline and string a

stop bead to the middle. Go through the bead again in the same direction to anchor it.
[2] String 24 cylinder beads. Turn, go through the second bead from the needle (**figure 1, a–b**), and work across the row in peyote stitch (Basics, p. 5) using cylinders until you reach the stop bead (**b–c**).
[3] Without picking up a new bead, go back through the last cylinder strung. Pick up a cylinder and work

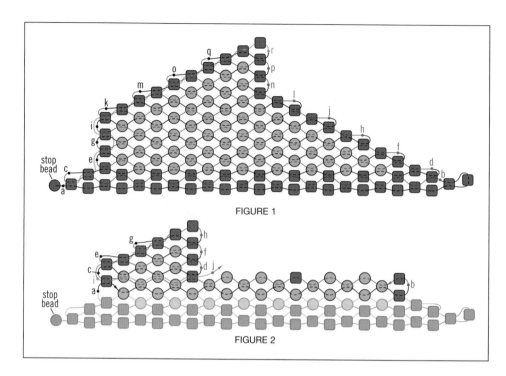

FIGURE 1

FIGURE 2

the next stitch. Work the next eight stitches using 11º seed beads in a mix of colors. Pick up a cylinder to make the last stitch (c–d).

[4] Without picking up a new bead, go back through the last cylinder. Pick up a cylinder and work one peyote stitch. Work the next eight stitches using 11ºs to complete the row (d–e).

[5] Pick up a cylinder and go back through the last 11º strung. Work the next seven stitches using 11ºs. Pick up a cylinder to make the last stitch (e–f).

[6] Without picking up a bead, go back through the last cylinder. Pick up a cylinder and go through the last 11º. Work the next seven stitches using 11ºs (f–g).

[7] Pick up a cylinder and go through the last 11º. Work the next six stitches using 11ºs. Pick up a cylinder to make the last stitch (g–h).

[8] Go back through the last cylinder again. Pick up a cylinder and go through the last 11º. Work the next six stitches using 11ºs (h–i).

[9] Pick up a cylinder and go through the last 11º. Work the next five stitches using 11ºs. Pick up a cylinder to make the last stitch (i–j).

[10] Without picking up a bead, go through the last cylinder. Pick up

a cylinder and go through the last 11º. Work the next four stitches using 11ºs. Pick up a cylinder to make the last stitch (j–k). The edge of the leaf will begin to change shape.

[11] Without picking up a bead, go through the last cylinder. Pick up a cylinder and go through the last 11º. Work the next three stitches using 11ºs. Pick up a cylinder to make the last stitch (k–l).

[12] Without stringing a bead, go through the last cylinder. Pick up a cylinder and go through the last 11º. Work two stitches using 11ºs. Pick up a cylinder to make the last stitch (l–m).

[13] Without picking up a bead, go through the last cylinder. Pick up a cylinder and go through the last 11º. Work the next two stitches using 11ºs (m–n).

[14] Pick up a cylinder and go through the last 11º. Work the next stitch using an 11º. Pick up a cylinder to make the last stitch (n–o). The edge of the leaf will change again.

[15] Without picking up a bead, go through the last cylinder. Work a cylinder and an 11º (o–p).

[16] Pick up a cylinder and go

through the last 11º. End the row with a cylinder (p–q).

[17] Without picking up a bead, go through the last cylinder. Pick up a cylinder to make the only stitch (q–r).

[18] Pick up a cylinder and go through the last cylinder. Continue through the diagonal row of cylinders along the edge of the leaf and weave in and out of the last few cylinders, exiting the first one (r–a). Don't cut the tail.

[19] Remove the stop bead and thread the needle on this tail. Starting with step 3, stitch the leaf's second half as the mirror image of the first.

Leaf variation

Complete steps 1–4 of the basic leaf, then follow the steps below.

[1] Pick up a cylinder and go through the last 11º strung. Work the next eight stitches using 11ºs to complete the row (figure 2, a–b).

[2] Pick up a cylinder and go through the last 11º. Work the next two stitches using 11ºs, then a cylinder. Repeat, then finish the row with two 11ºs (b–c).

[3] Pick up a cylinder and go through the last 11º strung.

FIGURE 3

MATERIALS

brooch

- 50g size 11º seed beads, two or more fall colors
- 10g Japanese cylinder beads, **1 or more** fall colors
- 10g size 5º hex cuts
- **12 or more** assorted beads, 2–12mm
- Nymo B or D or Fireline 6-lb. test
- beading needles, #12
- 24-gauge wire
- pin back

PEYOTE

Work two stitches using 11ºs (c–d). Your thread will be exiting a cylinder.

[4] Pick up a cylinder, turn, and go back through the last 11º strung. This begins to define one notch on the leaf's edge. Work the last two stitches using an 11º and a cylinder (d–e).

[5] Without picking up a bead, go through the last cylinder strung. Pick up a cylinder and an 11º to complete the row (e–f).

[6] Pick up a cylinder and go through the last 11º strung. Pick up a cylinder to make the end stitch (f–g).

[7] Without picking up a bead, go through the last cylinder strung. Complete the row, ending with a cylinder (g–h).

[8] Pick up a cylinder and go through the last cylinder strung. Continue through the diagonal row of cylinders along the edge of the leaf (h–i). Go through the next cylinder along the edge and work across to the cylinder at **point j.**

[9] Repeat steps 3–8 twice on this edge of the leaf. When the three

sections are complete, work back to the cylinder next to the stop bead. Remove the stop bead and thread the needle on the long tail. You'll use the short tail to sew the leaf to the base.

[10] To stitch the other half of the leaf, repeat steps 3–4 of the basic leaf, then repeat steps 1–9 of this variation.

Leaf base

[1] Make a seven-bead ladder using 5º hex cuts (Basics and **figure 3, a–b**). Work in brick stitch (Basics) for five rows, decreasing to two beads (b–c).

[2] Repeat the rows of brick stitch on the other edge of the ladder.

[3] With your thread exiting one of the two end beads, pick up nine 11ºs. Go under the thread bridge above the edge bead in the previous row (c–d). Go back through the last 11º.

[4] Pick up eight 11ºs and continue as in step 3 (d–e). Repeat around the base until you reach the starting point. Weave in the tails and trim the ends.

Assembly

My brooch uses four basic leaves and two with variations.

[1] Sew the stem end of each leaf onto the center of the base with the remaining thread tails. Place the leaves so they overlap slightly and sew through the leaf and a base bead (**photo a**). Trim the tail. You'll hide any exposed threads in step 3.

[2] With the ends of the wire exiting toward the front of the leaf, center a 6-in. (15cm) length of wire through a base bead or two. String a mix of beads on the wire and bend the ends into decorative shapes (**photo b**).

[3] Sew an assortment of beads in the center of the leaves to embellish them and hide the joins (**photo c**).

[4] Stitch a pin back to the back of the leaf base (**photo d**). ●

Circuitry collar

Make a space-age necklace with these
exquisite bezeling techniques

by **Laura Jean McCabe**

Originally created for the 2001 International Miyuki Beadwork Challenge, this neckpiece combines matte and luster beads with bezeled computer circuitry board and an ammonite to create a space-age aesthetic. On a conceptual level, the use of a computer circuitry board refers to the information age's never-ending quest for more memory.

For those interested in a less space-age look, these directions can easily be adapted to buttons or cabochons. If you use cabochons instead of circuitry board discs, skip the first section.

Cut the circuitry discs

[1] Locate a computer circuitry board. Mine was extracted from an old computer on its way to the trash.
[2] The disc shapes can be cut with a jeweler's saw, but this is very time consuming. The best way is to use a 1-in. (2.5cm) plug-cutting drill bit on a drill press. Be sure to wear safety goggles. Place the circuitry board on a scrap block of wood and slowly lower the drill to cut out the disc. Sand the discs with fine sandpaper to remove the rough edges.

Make the bezels

[1] Apply a thin coat of glue to the back of each disc or stone with a toothpick, and center it on a square of leather or Ultrasuede (photo a). Allow the glue to dry.
[2] Thread a needle with 4 ft. (1.2m) of waxed Nymo. Tie a knot at the end of the thread. Stitch through the

leather from the back, exiting at the disc's edge.
[3] Stitch a circle of beads as a base row around the disc with beaded backstitch as follows: Pick up six color B cylinder beads. Position the beads along the disc's edge and stitch through the leather to the back. Sew up through the leather between the third and fourth beads strung (photo b). Go through the last three beads again. Repeat around the disc. Adjust the bead count in the last stitch to ensure an even number of beads. Sew through all the beads a second time to smooth out the circle.
[4] Begin to stitch a circular, even-count peyote bezel (Basics) from the base row. Add rows as follows:
Rows 2–3: color B cylinder beads
Row 4: color B size 15º seed beads
Row 5: color A size 15º seed beads
Row 6: color D size 15º seed beads
[5] After the sixth row, sew back through the beads to the base row, and go through the leather. Knot the thread twice on the back, but don't cut it.

Make the bezel halos

[1] Backstitch a row of color G cylinder beads outside of the base row (photo c). This row should also have an even number of beads.
[2] Sew through the beads in this row a second time. Stitch through the leather, and knot the thread at the back. If you are using cabochons, trim the thread.

[3] If you are using computer circuitry discs, you may have circular holes in some of the discs. You can fill these holes with pearl fringe embellishments. Sew up through the hole, stringing a pearl that fits in the hole and a seed bead. Sew back through the pearl and the leather. Knot the thread and trim it.
[4] Thread a needle with 4 ft. of waxed Nymo. Tie a knot at the end of the thread. Stitch through the leather from the back, coming out between the base row and the halo's base row.
[5] Use E6000 to glue a second piece of leather to the back of the bezeled disc. After the glue dries, trim both leather layers to the shape of the disc (photo d). Be careful to not cut threads in the outer base row.
[6] Sew through both layers of leather to the back. Overhand stitch around the edge of the two layers (photo e).
[7] Sew up to the front of the bezel. Go through a couple of beads in the halo's base row. Add two more rows of circular even-count peyote stitch, as follows:
Row 2: color A cylinder beads
Row 3: color A size 11º seed beads
[8] Zigzag through the beads to secure the thread, ending in the base row. Sew to the back of the bezel, and trim the thread close to the leather.
[9] Make bezels and halos on all the discs and the centerpiece stone. Adapt the number of rows and the bead sizes to suit the centerpiece.

Assemble the necklace

[1] Arrange the pieces on your work space with the centerpiece stone in the middle and six discs on each side. Set aside the last disc to serve as the clasp.

[2] Thread a needle with 10 ft. (3m) of waxed and doubled Nymo. Sew through several beads in the outermost halo row of the first disc, leaving a 6–8 in. (15–20cm) tail to weave in later.

[3] Pick up a medium-shade pearl, a color A 11º, a medium-shade pearl, and three color A 15ºs. String the clasp hook over the 15ºs. String a medium-shade pearl, a color A 11º, and a medium-shade pearl. Skip two up beads on the halo's outside row, and sew through the third bead (**photo f**).

[4] To add three-branch fringes between up beads on the outer row, string a B 11º, 10–20 15ºs, a pearl (alternate medium and dark pearls), and three C 15ºs. Sew back through the pearl so the 15ºs form a picot (**photo g**). Sew back through four or five seed beads on the fringe and add another four or five-bead branch with a pearl and picot tip. Repeat to add a third branch. Sew back to the halo's outside row and through the next up bead in the row (**photo h**).

[5] Continue adding branched fringes between the up beads on the halo's outer row until the bottom third of the disc is fringed. Substitute E 15ºs for the B 15ºs on every third or fourth fringe.

[6] Pick up a medium-shade pearl, and sew through a bead on the outer row of the next disc (**photo i**).

[7] Repeat steps 4–6 and repeat the above until all the discs and the centerpiece stone are connected.

[8] Add a second hook clasp to the neckpiece's opposite end as in step 3.

[9] To embellish the top of the discs with pearl fringes, pick up a B 11º, a pale-shade pearl, an A 11º, and three F 15ºs. Sew back through the A bead, the pearl, and the B bead, forming a picot with the 15ºs (**photo j**). Sew through the next up bead on the outside row and repeat.

[10] Add pearl fringes to the top third of the disc. Pick up a medium-shade pearl and sew through a bead on the outside row of the next disc, three up beads above where the first pearl join was made (**photo k**).

[11] Repeat step 10 to join and embellish the top of the neckpiece. Weave in any remaining thread tails.

[12] To make the clasp disc, repeat step 2. String a B 11º and nine E 15ºs. String the eye portion of one clasp over the 15ºs and sew back through the 11º and over one up bead on the outside row.

[13] Repeat step 4 to add branched fringe around two-thirds of the disc.

[14] String the eye portion of the second clasp as in step 12.

[15] Add pearl fringes as in step 9 between the remaining beads on the outer row. Weave in any threads and trim the tails. ●

MATERIALS
necklace

- **13** 1-in. (2.5cm) round pieces of computer circuitry board or 1-in. round cabochons (matched dichroic glass sets available from Mrs. Magpie's, 610-433-6814)
- pyritized ammonite or other space-age stone, approximately 1½ x 1 in. (3.8 x 2.5cm)
- freshwater pearls:
  4 16-in. (41cm) strands 3mm buttons, dark green
  4 16-in. strands 4mm rounds, sage green
  3 16-in. strands 5mm rounds, pale green
- Japanese seed beads, size 11º:
  24g chartreuse gold luster, color A
  8g matte metallic copper, color B
- Japanese seed beads, size 15º:
  8g chartreuse gold luster, color A
  64g matte metallic copper, color B
  16g aqua/magenta lined, color C
  8g metallic olive, color D
  24g copper gold luster, color E
  8g topaz/green lined, color F
- Japanese cylinder beads, size 11º:
  16g chartreuse gold luster, color A
  16g matte metallic copper, color B
  16g sage gold luster, color G
- **28** 2 x 2-in. (5 x 5cm) squares of soft leather or Ultrasuede
- **2** silver hook-and-eye clasps
- Nymo D or Fireline fishing line, 6-lb. test
- beading needles, #13
- beeswax
- E6000 adhesive
- toothpicks

BRICK

Diamond and arch bracelet

Alternate increasing and decreasing brick stitch for a bold look

by **Anna Nehs**

The traditional way to make a brick stitch project is to start with the widest part and then decrease from there. But that approach isn't practical for this bracelet with its string of graduated diamonds, so instead it's made with both increases and decreases. Finish it with flowing crystal loops and a peyote clasp for a beautiful accessory you'll love to wear.

Start at one end and work increasing and decreasing brick stitch for the length of the bracelet, then add a clasp and embellishments. This bracelet is 7½ in. (19cm) long, including the clasp. Add or omit sections to fit it to your wrist.

Brick stitch band

Cut a 5-yd. (4.6m) length of thread. You will start working at the middle, so you will be using only half the thread's length at a time.

Increasing

See the Basics section, p. 5, for brick stitch instructions. Note that when you increase at the beginning of a row, the first two beads share the first bridge of thread from the previous row. The beads in the middle of the row are each connected to their own thread bridges, and the last two beads, although added separately, share the last thread bridge on the row below.

[1] Pick up two color A cylinder beads. Go back through the two beads again and through the first bead a third time (**photo a**).

[2] Pick up an A and a color B cylinder bead. Go under the thread bridge between the two beads in the previous row (**photo b**). Go back through the B. Pick up an A and go under the thread bridge between the beads in the previous row. This bridge may be hard to see since it is shared with the first two beads added. Then go back through the new A (**figure 1**).

[3] Pick up an A and a B. Go under the thread bridge between the first two beads in the previous row. Go back up the new B. Pick up a B and go under the thread bridge between the second and third beads in the

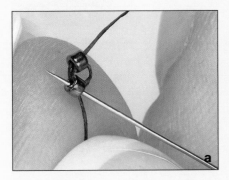

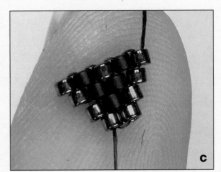

previous row, then go back through the new B. Pick up an A and go under the thread bridge between the second and third beads in the previous row. Go back through the new A (**figure 2**).
[4] Add the next row as described above, alternating As and Bs until you have a row of five beads (**photo c**).

Decreasing
When decreasing, you add two beads at the start of the row, but the first two beads share the second bridge of thread from the previous row instead of the first. Then each bead is added individually to the end of the row. The first two beads in a decrease row have to be anchored to each other to ensure proper placement. Since the first and last beads in the row have

their own thread bridges, the result is that the new row is one bead shorter than the previous row.
[1] With the thread exiting the last bead in the row, pick up an A and a B.
[2] Go under the thread bridge between the second and third beads from the previous row (**photo d**, p. 52). Go back up through the B, down through the A, and back up the B (**figure 3, a–b**).
[3] Pick up a B and go under the thread bridge between the next two beads on the previous row. Go back through the new B (**b–c**). Pick up an A and go under the last thread bridge in the previous row. Go back through the new A (**c–d**).
[4] Pick up an A and a B and repeat step 2. Pick up an A and go under the

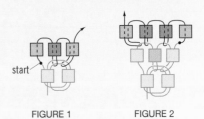

FIGURE 1   FIGURE 2

thread bridge between the last two beads in the previous row. Go back through the new A (**d–e**).
[5] Pick up two As and repeat step 2.
[6] Make every odd-numbered diamond like the first diamond. Make the second diamond six beads wide at the center, the fourth diamond seven beads wide, the sixth diamond eight beads wide, and the eighth diamond nine beads wide, following the color

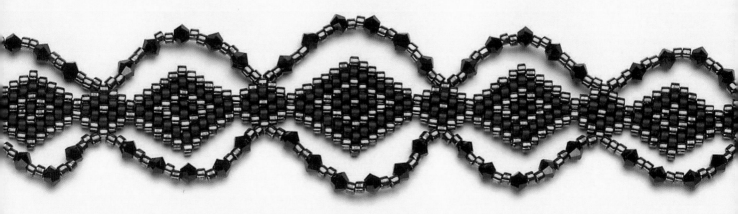

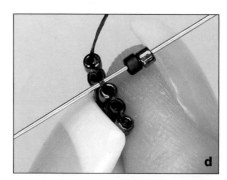

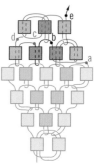

MATERIALS
bracelet 7½ in. (19cm)
- Japanese cylinder beads
  4g, metallic gold, color A
  4g, matte black, color B
- **60** 3mm bicone crystals
- Nymo D beading thread
- button or flat bead for clasp
- beading needles, #12

pattern of the bracelet on p. 50-51. Then decrease the width of the even-numbered diamonds to mirror the first half of the bracelet. End with an odd-numbered diamond.

Clasp

[1] When the last section of the bracelet is completed, the needle will exit one of the As on the last row. Make a section of brick stitch large enough to accommodate a button or a flat bead with a hole in the middle, using Bs. This one is six beads across the widest row (**photo e**).

[2] Stitch the button to the middle of the brick stitch section. Tie off the thread using half-hitch knots (Basics), and trim.

[3] Thread the needle on the tail at the other end, and make an odd-numbered loop of Bs that will fit around the button. Go through the other A and back through the first A and the first loop bead.

[4] Weave one A between every other B in the loop (peyote stitch, Basics) to add strength and stability (**photo f**). Reinforce the loop by going through all the beads at least one more time.

Crystal loops

[1] Position the needle so it exits the edge bead of the middle row of the first small diamond.

[2] Alternate two or three As with three crystals to make the first arch. Then go through the edge bead on the middle row of the next small diamond (**photo g**). You'll have to change the number of As to adjust the size of the arches as the diamonds between them get larger. As you work toward the center, each arch has one more crystal than the previous one has.

[3] Repeat steps 1–2 on the other side of the bracelet. Tie off the tails and trim the thread. ●

FIGURE 3

Starlight, star bright earrings

Brick stitch earrings shine day or night

by **Sharon McCauley**

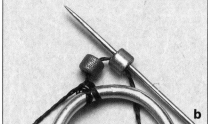

These earrings are so quick and easy to stitch you'll find you can't stop after making just one pair. They provide a wonderful way to showcase vintage buttons without damaging them, or to highlight flat, button-shaped beads.

Foundation row

[1] Use a lark's head knot (Basics, p. 5) to fasten 24 in. (61cm) of Nymo to a jump ring (**photo a**), leaving a 4-in. (10cm) tail.
[2] Attach a beading needle to one of the threads and pick up a color A and a color B cylinder bead. Go through the ring and sew through the B (**photo b**).
[3] Pick up a C, go through the ring, and back through the C (**photo c**). Work another C and a B.
[4] Repeat the sequence three times. Sew down through the first A picked up in step 2, go through the ring, and go back up through the A (**photo d**).

Points

[1] Pick up an A and a B, and work a brick stitch (Basics and **photo e**). Then work two Cs and a B. Increase

with an A. To increase, work the A on the same thread bridge as the B (**photo f**). Turn the piece after each row.
Row 3: A, B, C, B, A (**photo g**).
Row 4: A, B, B, A.
Row 5: A, B, A.
Row 6: A, A (**photo h**).
[2] Pick up three size 15º seeds and go through the adjacent A (**photo i**) to make a picot.
[3] Sew through the As along the edge, and go through the A on the foundation row (**photo j**). Go through the ring and back through the A.
[4] Repeat steps 1–3 three more times, but on the last point, end with step 2.

Earring finding

[1] Go through the adjacent A and exit the top picot bead (**photo k**). Pick up three 15ºs, an earring finding, and three 15ºs.
[2] Go through the same 15º your thread is exiting in the opposite direction to form a loop (**photo l**).
[3] Retrace the thread path for security.

Button or bead

The width of the the button's shank or irregularities in 15ºs may cause variations in the number of 15ºs needed to lock the button in place, so adjust these instructions as needed. A flat bead with a single hole in the center also can be used.

Adding a flat bead

[1] Weave through the stitches and exit the second C on the foundation row (**photo m**).
[2] Pick up three 15ºs and go through the hole in the bead. Pick up a 15º and go back through the hole. Pick up three more 15ºs. Go through the corresponding C on the opposite side of the ring (**photo n**).
[3] Weave through the foundation beads. Exit the second C of the next sequence and repeat step 2 (**photo o**).

Adding a shank button

[1] Start as in step 1 of "Adding a flat bead."
[2] Pick up two or more 15ºs, go through the shank, and pick up two or more additional 15ºs. Go through

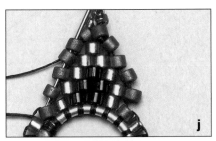

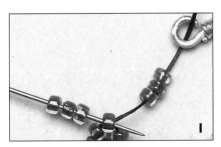

the corresponding C on the opposite side of the ring.

[3] Follow step 3 of "Adding a flat bead."

Embroidery

[1] Pick up a 15º and go under the thread that holds one of the foundation row beads in place (**photo p**). Pick up a 15º and sew under the thread of the next foundation row bead. Embroider a bead to each thread of the foundation row.

[2] Go through all the embroidered beads again and then weave through several brick-stitched beads. Make a half-hitch knot (Basics) and dot with glue. When dry, weave through several beads and trim. Repeat with any other tails.

Crystal embellishment

Secure an 18-in. (46cm) length of thread in the beadwork and exit at point a in **figure 1**. Pick up a 6mm crystal and three 15ºs, and go back through the crystal. Sew into the earring at point b.

FIGURE 1

Fringe

[1] Secure an 18-in. (46cm) length of thread in the beadwork and exit at point c, d, or e on figure 1. Pick up ten 15ºs, a flower bead, and a drop. Go back through the flower and three 15ºs.

[2] Pick up three 15ºs, a drop, and three 15ºs. Skip a 15º on the stem and go through the next two 15ºs.

[3] Repeat step 2, but go through the rest of the 15ºs on the stem and sew through the beadwork to exit at another fringe point.

[4] Repeat the steps above to make additional fringe, but make the other two fringes shorter and include only one branch on each. ◗

MATERIALS

pair of earrings

- 1g Japanese cylinder beads, each of **3** colors
- 1g size 15º seed beads
- **2** buttons or flat beads, ½ in. (1.3cm) diameter
- **2** 10mm soldered jump rings
- pair of earring findings
- Nymo D conditioned with Thread Heaven
- beading needles, #12

optional crystal points

- **8** 6mm bicone crystals

optional fringe

- **6** Czech glass flowers
- **14** drop beads

BRICK

Cones of many colors

Add a distinctive brick-stitch finding to your design repertoire

by **Ann Egan**

Finish a luxurious multistrand necklace with brick-stitch cones for a truly unique look. Stitched in two-drop brick stitch, these cones are an easy way to add a designer touch. Be sure you're familiar with regular brick stitch (Basics, p. 5) before you begin. These cones are more than functional; they're decorative elements, so position them to hang in front. These are about 6 in. (15cm) from the clasp.

Brick-stitch cones

[1] Following either pattern on p. 57 or your own design, start these cones with a ladder (Basics) using two beads per stitch for 23 stitches (**figure 1**). Zigzag back through the ladder to reinforce it (**figure 2**).

[2] Work the next 19 rows in two-drop brick stitch (**figure 3**), decreasing one stitch in each row. The last row will have four pairs of beads.

[3] With your thread exiting the edge bead on the last row, go down through the two beads on the opposite edge and back up the two beads on the first side. Repeat to strengthen the seam. Continue sewing the long sides of the triangle together (**figure 4**), treating each two-bead stack as a single bead. Make an extra pass through the last pairs of beads, secure the thread in the beadwork with a few half-hitch knots (Basics), and trim the tails.

[4] Make a second cone to match the first.

Beaded strands

[1] Center a needle on a 1.3 yd. (1.2m) length of thread. Working with doubled thread, transfer 18 in. (46cm) of beads from the hank onto doubled stringing cord, leaving a 5-in. (13cm) tail on each end of the new strand. Tape the ends to keep the beads from sliding off.

[2] Continue stringing until you have enough strands to fill the cones. (These necklaces have 36 strands of size 15º seed beads, but you can use fewer strands if you work with larger beads.) Gather the tails at one end and secure them with an overhand knot (Basics) close to the beads (**photo a**). Repeat on the other

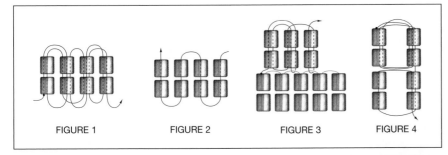

FIGURE 1   FIGURE 2   FIGURE 3   FIGURE 4

a   b

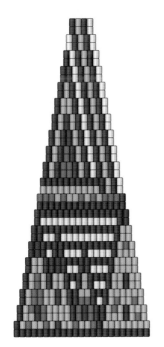

c

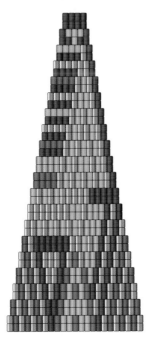

d

MATERIALS
cones and beaded strands
- 2–3 hanks seed beads, size
  11º or smaller
- small amounts of Japanese
  cylinder beads, size 11º, in **7** colors
- **2** small flat spacer beads
- **2** head pins or 6 in. (15cm)
  20-gauge half-hard wire
- Nymo D, Fireline, or other
  beading thread
- beading needles, #10
- G-S Hypo Cement
- 6 in. (15cm) yarn
- Stringth, Power Pro, Fireline, or
  other beading cord
- twisted wire or Big-Eye needles

finishing
- 12 in. (30cm) assorted beads
  to complement cones
- flexible beading wire, .013 or
  .014, or medium-gauge wire
- **2** crimp beads (if using
  beading wire)
- clasp
- crimping pliers
- roundnose pliers
- wire cutters

BRICK

end. Allow a little ease so the beads hang freely.

[3] Turn a small wrapped loop at the end of each head pin (Basics) or 3-in. (7.6cm) length of wire. Tie each group of tails onto a loop with a surgeon's knot (Basics and **photo b**). Glue the knots and trim the tails.

Attaching strands to cones

[1] Stuff a piece of yarn into the cone's tip to give it body.

[2] Insert the wire's straight end into the cone and out the hole at the top (**photo c**). If the loop distorts the cone, pinch the loop into an oval.

[3] Slip a small bead or spacer onto the wire, then make a small

wrapped loop as close as possible to the spacer (**photo d**).

[4] Repeat these steps with the other cone.

Completing the necklace

For the span between the cones and clasp, use a colorful mix of beads that complements the cones. For example, string gemstones, Bali silver, and bugles on flexible beading wire, then crimp (Basics) one end to the wrapped loop above a cone and the other to the clasp (turquoise necklace). Or, try stitching an assortment of beaded beads and stringing them on short lengths of wire. Then make wrapped loops at the ends of the wires and link them into a graceful chain (black necklace). Add beads or silver spacers, as desired. ●

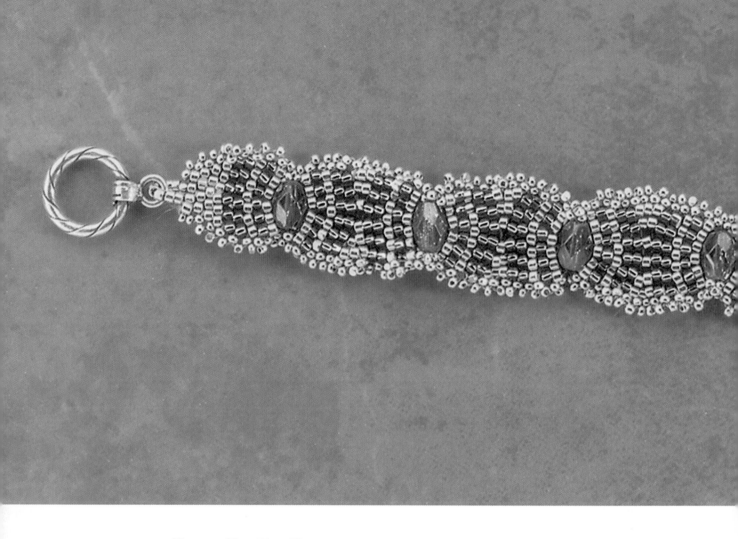

Gold-brick bracelet

Circle your wrist with golden links

by **Glenda Payseno**

Add a regal touch to your wardrobe with a rich-looking accessory. This bracelet is made from a series of brick-stitch links joined by cylinder-bead segments. A fire-polished faceted bead forms the core of each link and determines the width of the bracelet. Tightly woven brick-stitch rows fan out from each faceted bead. The length of the bracelet is determined by the number of links joined together. A glimmering picot trim embellishes the edges.

Make the links

Ladder stitch usually forms the base row for brick stitch, but with the links in this bracelet, you anchor cylinder beads to a thread that runs through the faceted bead. Work with 18-in. (46cm) lengths of purple or black conditioned thread (Basics, p. 5).

[1] **Base row:** Leave a 5-in. (13cm) tail and go through a fire-polished bead. Go through the bead again in the same direction, and tie the tail and working thread together with a surgeon's knot (Basics). Tie the knot close to the hole at one end of the bead (**figure 1**).

[2] Pick up two cylinder beads, pull the thread tight, and go under both threads that are wrapped around the faceted bead (**photo a**). Go up

through the last bead strung (**photo b**) and down through the first bead. Come up through the last bead again. Pick up another bead, go under the threads, and exit the bead just added. Repeat for a total of six cylinders, ending with the thread exiting from the last bead picked up (**photo c**). Turn your work.

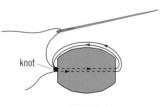

knot

FIGURE 1

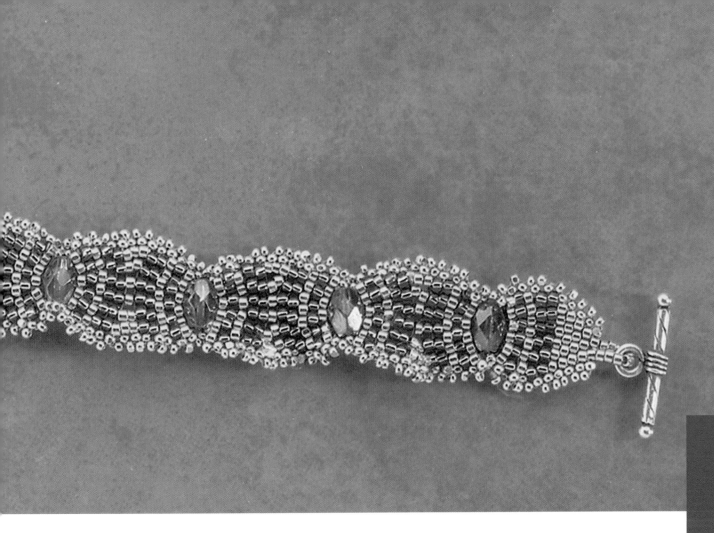

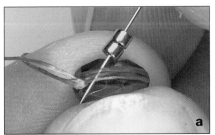

a

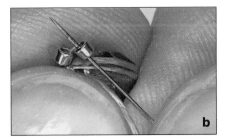

b

c

[3] **Row 2:** Work in brick stitch (Basics) with size 11º seed beads. For the second stitch, make an increase between the second and third cylinders of the first row by attaching the increase bead to the same loop as the previous stitch (Basics and **photo d**, p. 60). There are a total of six seeds in this row. Turn your work.

[4] **Row 3:** Work in brick stitch using cylinder beads. Make an increase between the second and third beads of the previous row and another between the fourth and fifth beads for a total of seven cylinders. Turn.

[5] **Row 4:** Work a row of 11º seeds in brick stitch for a total of six beads.

[6] **Row 5:** Repeat row 2 (six beads). Do not weave in the thread end; use it later to join the links or to weave the end rows of the bracelet. This completes one side of a link (**photo e**).

[7] Start a new thread and repeat steps 1–6 on the other side of the fire-polished bead. **Photo f** shows one complete link.

[8] Repeat steps 1–7 to make seven more links.

Join the links

[1] Begin with a thread that exits from the topmost bead on one link.

Pick up three cylinder beads and go through the two edge beads on another link (**figure 2, a–b**).

[2] Go through the next two beads, pick up two cylinders, and go though the corresponding beads on the first link (**b–c**).

[3] Go through the next two beads, pick up one cylinder, and go through the corresponding beads on the other link (**c–d**).

[4] Repeat step 3 (**d–e**), step 2 (**e–f**), and step 1 (**f–g**).

[5] Repeat steps 1–4 to join the remaining links.

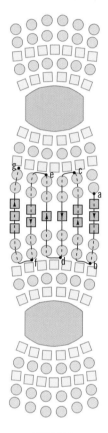

Finish the ends

[1] Thread a needle on the long tail remaining at one edge. Work in brick stitch and make one increase between the second and third seeds of the last row (six beads). Turn.

[2] Work four more rows of brick stitch until two cylinders remain. Pick up four cylinders, the toggle bar, and four more cylinders. Weave down into the row of two cylinders, then retrace this thread path several times for added security (**figure 3, a–b**).

[3] Repeat steps 1–2 at the other end of the bracelet with the clasp loop.

Add a picot edge

Use size 13º tri-cut beads to make a picot edge along both sides of the bracelet. Use 24-in. (61cm) lengths of gold-colored conditioned thread.

[1] Begin at one end of the bracelet with the thread exiting the end cylinder (**figure 4, point a**). Pick up three tri-cut beads and go under the thread between the first cylinders in rows 4 and 3 (**figure 4, point b**). Come up through the last tri-cut added.

[2] Pick up two tri-cuts and go under the thread between the next two cylinders (**figure 4, point c**). Come up through the last tri-cut added.

MATERIALS
bracelet 7½ in. (19cm)
- 8 6mm fire-polished beads
- 4g Japanese cylinder beads, gold-plated
- 8g size 11º Japanese seed beads, purple
- hank size 13º or 14º tri-cut seed beads, gold plated
- toggle clasp
- Nymo D in purple or black and gold
- beeswax or Thread Heaven
- beading needles, #12
- G-S Hypo Cement

[3] Repeat step 2 six times.

[4] When you reach a fire-polished bead, pick up two tri-cuts, go under the thread at the edge of the fire-polished bead, and go through the last tri-cut. Pick up two tri-cuts, go under the thread on the other edge of the fire-polished bead, and go through the last tri-cut (**photo g**). Continue making picots along the length of the bracelet.

[5] Repeat steps 1–4 on the other side of the bracelet.

Finishing

When finished, weave all thread tails back and forth through several beads to secure, dab with a dot of glue, and clip the thread close to the beads. ●

FIGURE 3

FIGURE 2

FIGURE 4

Woven geometrics

Create bold shapes with peyote and brick stitch

by **Nicole Schlinger**

Since brick and peyote stitches have a similar appearance, but are worked differently, they make natural partners in pieces where the stitching needs to change directions. Such is the case in the woven bracelet and necklace shown here.

start

FIGURE 1

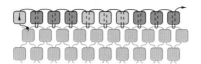

FIGURE 2

start

FIGURE 3

FIGURE 4

a

b

Bracelet

Measure your hand at the widest part (**photo a**) to determine the length needed to slide on the bracelet. Use 24-in. (61cm) lengths of Nymo. Trim the threads only when instructed.

Peyote strip

[**1**] Pick up one color B bead and three color A beads, leaving a 9-in. (27cm) tail.
[**2**] Work in peyote (Basics, p. 5), picking up a B along one edge until the strip is the length determined above. The number of edge beads must be divisible by six. **Photo b** shows the strip in process.
[**3**] Make a second strip.

Brick-stitch outline row

[**1**] Working with the color B edge at the bottom, secure a new thread so it exits the top left A.
[**2**] Pick up a B and an A. Work in brick stitch (Basics), using the thread bridge between the second and third beads on the peyote strip (**figure 1**). Work two brick stitches using As.
[**3**] Work three Bs and three As. Repeat this sequence (**figure 2**) to the end of the strip, ending with two Bs.
[**4**] Repeat steps 1–3 with the other strip.

Diagonal panels

All the diagonals on a strip slant in the same direction. Turn the piece after you complete each row of brick stitch.
[**1**] Hold one strip so the color B edge is at the bottom and secure a new thread. Exit the first brick-stitched B at the top.
[**2**] Working in brick stitch, pick up a B and an A. Then work two As and a B (**photo c**). Turn the piece.
[**3**] Pick up a B and an A. Increase at the beginning of the row (**figure 3**). Work two As and a B (**photo d**).
[**4**] Pick up a B and an A. Work two As and a B increase at the end of the row (**figure 4**).
[**5**] Repeat steps 2–4 for a total of 17 rows.
[**6**] To begin the next and all subsequent diagonals, start a new thread. Exit the third B on the brick-stitch outline. Repeat steps 2–5 across the strip. **Photo e** shows the spacing of the diagonals.
[**7**] Repeat on the other strip.

Connect the diagonals

Use the thread tail to sew the beads of the end row of a diagonal over the corresponding beads on the brick-stitch outline row.
[**1**] Position the strips so the solid color B edges are on the outsides (**figure 5**).
[**2**] Weave the diagonals on one strip through the diagonals on the other (**figure 5**). To connect the woven diagonals, line up the end row of a diagonal's beads over the outline row on the other strip (**figure 5, inset**).
[**3**] Using the thread tail exiting from the B on the diagonal, sew over to the corresponding B on the outline row. Go down through the B

(**photo f**) and up through the next A on the diagonal. Then sew over to the next A on the outline row. Connect the other beads on the diagonal to the outline row in the same way. **Photo g** shows a finished joint.
[**4**] Tie off the tail by working it through several beads. Tie a half-hitch knot (Basics). Dot the knot with glue. Sew through a few more beads and cut the thread.
[**5**] Repeat steps 2–4 to connect each diagonal along the length of the bracelet. Don't connect the last diagonals until the bracelet is formed into a circle.
[**6**] Repeat these steps to connect the diagonals on the other strip.

Finishing

[**1**] Use the tail to zip the ends of the peyote strips together (**figure 6, a–b**, p. 64).
[**2**] Secure the thread in the beadwork with half-hitch knots and trim the tail.
[**3**] Following the established pattern, weave and connect the remaining diagonals. Tie off the remaining tails.

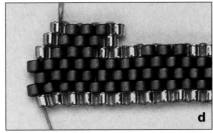

Necklace

Measure your neck to determine the length of your necklace. The beadwork on this one is 14½ in. (36cm). The clasp adds about another inch (2.5cm).

band

[1] Follow steps 1–2 of the peyote strip instructions for the bracelet. The final number of edge beads must be divisible by seven.

[2] Work steps 1–2 of the brick stitch outline instructions. Then work a repeating pattern of four Bs and three As across the row.

First leg

[1] Work steps 1–4 of the diagonal panel instructions for a total of 11 rows.

[2] Pick up two As and increase at the beginning of the row. Work two As and a B (**figure 7, row 12**).

[3] Pick up a B and an A. Then work two As and an A increase (**row 13**).

[4] Repeat step 2 (**row 14**).

[5] Pick up a B and an A. Then work two As and a B (**row 15**).

The point

[1] Pick up a B and an A. Work an A and a B (**row 16**).

[2] Pick up a B and an A, then a B (**row 17**).

[3] Pick up two Bs (**row 18**).

[4] Pick up a B, a fire-polished bead, and a B.

[5] Skip the B and retrace the thread path, but go through the B adjacent to the starting B (**figure 7, a–b**).

[6] Sew through the three Bs along the edge (**b–c**).

Second leg

[1] With the thread exiting the B, pick up a B and sew through the adjacent A. Then go through the B again (**figure 8, a–b**).

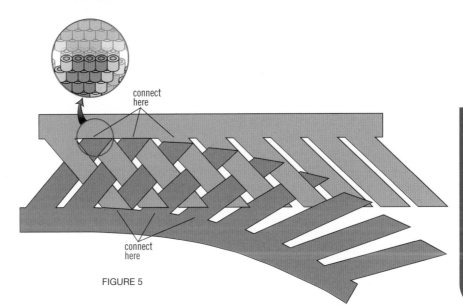

FIGURE 5

[2] Pick up a B and an A and increase at the beginning of the row. Sew through the adjacent A. Then go through two As diagonally and exit an A in the row above (**figure 9, a–b**).

[3] Work two As and a B increase at the end of the row.

[4] Pick up a B and an A and increase at the beginning of the row. Then work two As. Sew through the adjacent B and back through the last A added (**figure 10, a–b**).

[5] Pick up a B and an A and work a stitch on the thread bridge between the two As on the previous row (**figure 11, a–b**). Work two As and a B increase at the end of the row. This establishes the five-bead pattern for the second leg.

[6] Pick up a B and an A and work an increase at the beginning of the row. Work two As and a B.

[7] Pick up a B and an A. Work two As and a B increase at the end of the row.

[8] Repeat steps 6–7 three more times to complete the second leg (11 rows total). Do not connect the leg and do not cut the thread tail.

[9] Secure a new thread in the beadwork, and sew through beads to exit the third B past the previous leg. Repeat steps 1–8 to make Vs along the outline row. Do not start Vs after the last two B segments, as they will be used only as connection points for other Vs.

Connect the second leg

[1] Follow **figure 12** to interweave the legs of the Vs.

[2] Connect the tops of the Vs to the brick-stitch outline on the peyote strip as described in step 3 of the

BRICK

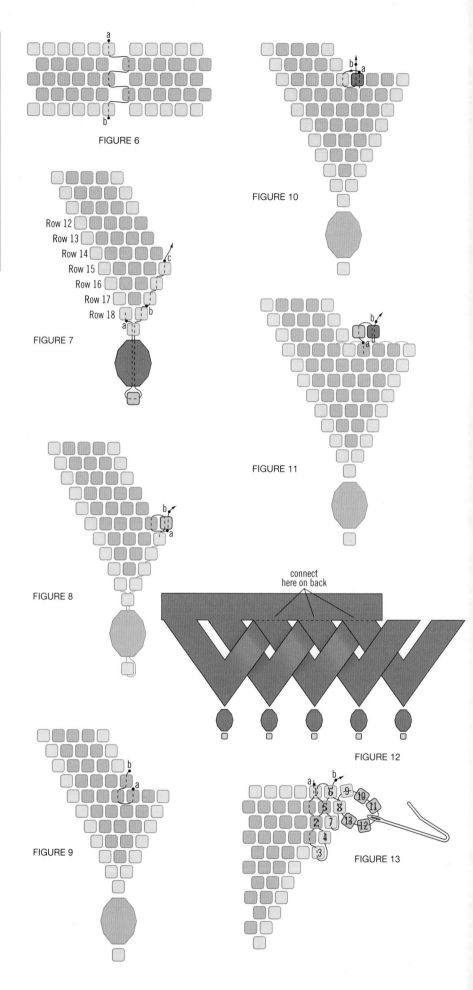

"connect the diagonals" instructions
for the bracelet.

[3] Carefully join the legs of the last
two Vs to the peyote strip in the
same manner.

Finishing

[1] Work in peyote, using the tail
remaining at either end of the
necklace. See **figure 13, beads 1–9**
for the sequence. Your sequence
may vary.

[2] Pick up two Bs (**beads 10 and
11**), one part of the clasp, and two
Bs (**beads 12 and 13**). Sew back into
the beads of the peyote strip. For
added security go though **beads 8–13**
several times.

[3] Weave back into the peyote strip,
tie a half-hitch knot, and dot with
glue. Weave through several more
beads and trim the tail.

[4] Repeat steps 1–3 at the other
end of the necklace with the other
clasp half.

[5] Tie off and weave in any
remaining tails. ●

FIGURE 6

FIGURE 7

FIGURE 8

FIGURE 9

FIGURE 10

FIGURE 11

FIGURE 12

FIGURE 13

LOOMWORK

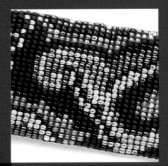

Loomwork basics

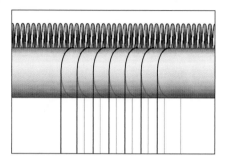

FIGURE 1

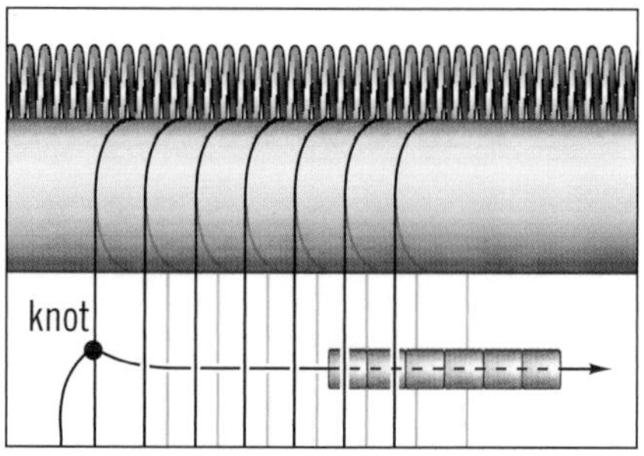

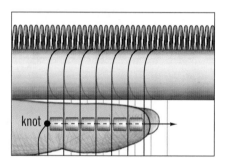

FIGURE 2

FIGURE 3

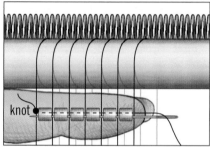

FIGURE 4

Set up the warp

[1] Tie the end of the spool of thread to the screw or hook at the top of the loom.

[2] Bring the thread over one spring and across to the spring at the other end of the loom. Wrap the thread around the screw or hook at the bottom of the loom. Bring the thread back over the springs, going toward the top of the loom.

[3] Continue wrapping the thread between springs, keeping the threads a bead's width apart, until you have one more warp thread than the number of beads in the width of the pattern (**figure 1**). Keep the tension even, but not too tight. Secure the last warp thread to a hook or screw on the loom, then cut the thread from the spool.

Weave the pattern

[1] Tie the end of a length of thread to the first warp thread just below the spring at the top of the loom. Bring the needle under the warp threads. String the first row of beads as shown on the pattern, and slide them to the knot (**figure 2**).

[2] Push the beads up between the warp threads with your finger (**figure 3**).

[3] Sew back through the beads, keeping the needle above the warp threads (**figure 4**). Repeat, following the pattern row by row.

[4] Once you complete the last row, secure the working thread by weaving it into the beadwork.

Paisley choker

Connect a cloth of beads with a bead-embroidered centerpiece

by **Dina Krieg**

You'll love the sensuous feel of this loomwork choker with a bead embroidered centerpiece. Use the same colors as shown in the choker above or adapt the pattern to your own colors.

After weaving the strips, embroider the beaded centerpiece. Then join the three pieces, positioning the loom-work strips so they mirror each other, line the entire piece with Ultrasuede, and attach a hook-and-eye clasp.

Loomwork

If your loom is long enough, you can weave both pieces on the same set of warp threads. But if you're using a smaller loom, you'll need to warp it separately for each piece. The two woven pieces are each 6¼ by 1⁷⁄₁₆ in. (16 x 3.8cm). You'll need a loom that can accommodate a warp at least 10 in. (25cm) long. To weave both pieces on one warp, the warp will need to be at least 24 in. (61cm) long.

[1] Set up your loom with 27 warp threads (Loomwork Basics, p. 66).
[2] Cut a 2–3-yd. (1.8–2.7m) length of black Nymo B and thread it in a Big Eye needle. Tie the end of the thread to the leftmost warp thread near one of the spring separators with the first half of a square knot (Basics, p. 5), leaving an 18-in. (46cm) tail. You'll untie the knot and weave in the tail thread later.
[3] Follow the chart on p. 69 to work the first loomed piece. To start, pick up the 26 beads of the first row from left to right. Pass the needle and thread under the warp threads, and position the beads so that one sits between each pair of warp threads. If you are left-handed, tie onto the right-hand warp thread, string from right to left, and weave back from left to right. Push up on the beads from below with the index finger of your non-dominant hand (**photo a**).

Pass the needle through the beads above the warp threads from right to left. Look for the glint of the needle above each warp thread to ensure that you are above the warps (**photo b**). Be careful not to split threads.
[4] Weave all the rows of the pattern as in step 3. Always string from left to right on the chart.

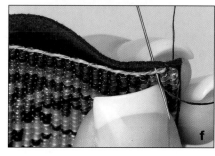

[5] Make another strip like the first.

[6] Before removing the loom work, weave the ending thread tail over and under alternating warp threads for 15–20 rows. This part will look like woven cloth. Secure the tail in the woven selvage with a few knots and trim. Then untie the starting knot and weave the starting tail like the ending tail.

[7] Wrap first-aid paper tape around both sides of the woven selvages so that they are slightly narrower than the beadwoven section. This makes a nice crisp edge to fold back under the weaving. Set the woven pieces aside.

Centerpiece

[1] Cut one piece each of Lacy's Stiff Stuff and Ultrasuede approximately 1½ x 2 in. (3.8 x 5cm). Baste the edges together. Mark a rectangle 18mm by 25mm (slightly smaller than ¾ x 1 in.) on the center of the Ultrasuede. (Baste around this area with white thread so you can see it

well.) Start filling in the rectangle with 3mm faceted beads. Start at the perimeter, sewing just inside the basted lines (**photo c**). Work in a circle toward the center. Do not crowd the beads too closely together or the backing will buckle. You want the piece to lie flat with the beads touching.

[2] When the area is filled in, alternate filling in the spaces between the 3mm beads with size 12º and 9º three-cut seed beads (**photo d**—green beads are used for clarity). Do not pull too tightly. If the seed beads don't fit between the 3mm beads, just let them sit on top of the beads. Make sure the thread doesn't show. Fill in the area randomly, working in different directions. You will now have three levels of randomly-placed beads of different sizes.

[3] Remove the basting thread and outline the perimeter with size 8º hex beads, using three-bead backstitch as follows: pickup three beads and

sew through the Ultrasuede right after the third bead. Come back up between the second and third beads, go through the third bead, and pick up three more beads (**photo e**). Repeat around.

[4] Trim the Ultrasuede close to the beads, taking care not to cut any of the threads used to sew the beads in place.

Connections

[1] Sew the loomed pieces to the centerpiece Ultrasuede and backing (**photo f**). Make sure the loomed pieces lie in a straight line.

[2] Now cut a single length of Ultrasuede the width of the loomed pieces and long enough to fit around your neck plus 2–2¼ in. (5–5.6cm).

[3] Position the Ultrasuede so it's even with the loomwork strip on one end and extends past the end of the other loomwork strip.

[4] Glue the Ultrasuede to the back of the centerpiece with E6000.

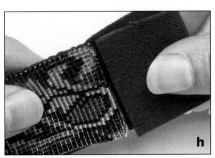

g

h

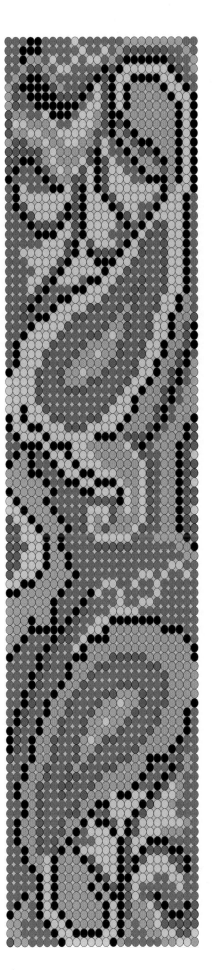

MATERIALS

choker 16 in. (41cm)

- **80-90** 3mm black fire-polished beads
- 1g size 8º hex beads
- 1g each size 12º and 9º 3-cut beads
- Japanese cylinder beads in following quantities:
  16g matte black
  11g shiny black
  7g galvanized or metallic gold
  6g bronze
  5g lavender
  3g dark purple
- Lacy's Stiff Stuff or heavy pellon interfacing
- black Ultrasuede
- black and white Nymo B
- black Nymo D for warp
- Big Eye needle
- E6000 glue
- 2 hook-and-eye closures
- first-aid paper tape (pharmacy)
- beadweaving loom

[5] Hand sew the loomwork to the Ultrasuede on all edges (**photo g**). Curve the piece very slightly while stitching so it will not buckle when worn.

[6] On the end with the excess Ultrasuede, fold the Ultrasuede back on itself so it is even with the edge of the loomwork (**photo h**). It should extend 1–1⅛ in. (2.5–3cm).

[7] Test the fit of the necklace, and determine approximately where the hook-and-eye closures should be placed. Sew the eyes in place on one end of the choker, then sew the hooks on the other end so the piece fits your neck perfectly. ●

Layered loomwork pendant

Use a woven pendant to highlight an art glass bead

by **Don Pierce**

This pendant was designed to create a simple showcase for an art glass bead. One of the problems with combining large, heavy beads with loomwork is how to carry the weight without distorting the loomwork. In this case, multiple layers of loomwork fold together to form a strong support.

You can make this piece as wide or as narrow as you like; just remember to warp your loom with one more warp thread than the number of beads in the widest section.

[1] Warp your loom (Loomwork Basics, p. 66) with Nymo and string 19 warp threads. Space your warp threads to match the width of the Japanese cylinder beads.

[2] Cut a 5-ft. (1.5m) length of Nymo for the weft thread and tie it to the far left warp thread with an overhand knot (Basics, p. 5 and **photo a**) leaving an 8-in. (20cm) tail. Thread a needle on the long end of the thread.

[3] The widest section is worked first. Pick up 18 color A beads for the first row, and pass the beads and thread under the warp threads.

[4] While holding the tension of the weft thread with your right hand, push the beads up between the warps with your left index finger. Bring the needle through the beads above the warp threads (**photo b**). Look for the shine of the needle between the beads to make sure the needle is above the warp threads.

[5] Add the next row as in steps 3–4. Continue until you have 44 rows. At some point you will need to add thread for your weft. When the thread becomes too short, pass the thread back through the previous row and tie an overhand knot around a warp thread. Do not trim the weft thread

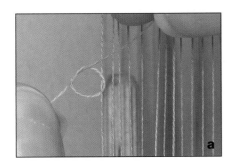

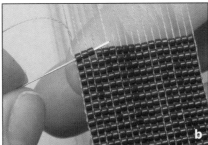

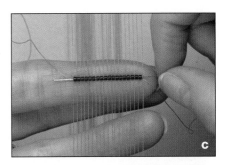

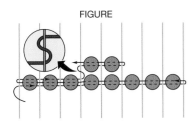

FIGURE

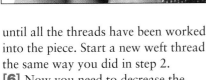

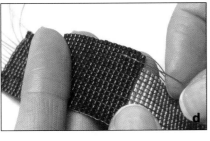

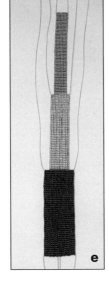

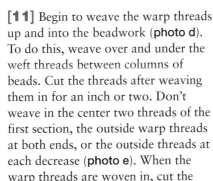
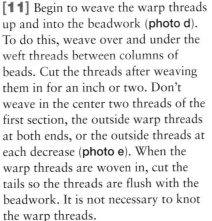

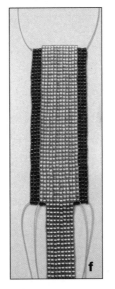

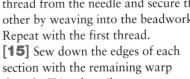

until all the threads have been worked into the piece. Start a new weft thread the same way you did in step 2.

[6] Now you need to decrease the next row by three beads on each side. Bring the needle up over the left edge warp thread and back through the last three beads (**photo c**).

[7] Position the weft thread under the fourth warp thread. Wrap the weft thread up over the top of the warp thread and back under it (**figure**).

[8] Pick up 12 color B beads. Bring the needle under the warps, bringing it up between the third and fourth warp threads from the right side. Repeat steps 4–5 until you have 44 rows in color B.

[9] Decrease two beads on each side, as in steps 6–7. Pick up eight color C beads for each row. This section has 57 rows.

[10] Weave the weft tails through the loomwork to secure them, and trim the excess threads. Cut the warp threads and remove the beadwork from the loom. You will want the top and bottom of the beadwork to have about 6-in. (15cm) warp tails.

[11] Begin to weave the warp threads up and into the beadwork (**photo d**). To do this, weave over and under the weft threads between columns of beads. Cut the threads after weaving them in for an inch or two. Don't weave in the center two threads of the first section, the outside warp threads at both ends, or the outside threads at each decrease (**photo e**). When the warp threads are woven in, cut the tails so the threads are flush with the beadwork. It is not necessary to knot the warp threads.

[12] Lay the beadwork out flat and apply a thin layer of glue or a strip of tape to the middle section. Fold the middle section onto the first section so the rows line up (**photo f**). Press it firmly into place, and allow it to dry.

[13] Apply a layer of glue or a strip of tape to all but the last 13 rows of the last section and fold it over the middle section. Once the glue is dry, bend the 13 extra rows toward the back of the beadwork, and stitch it securely to the end row of the first section using the end warp threads (**photo g**).

MATERIALS
pendant
- Japanese cylinder beads, size 11º, 5g each of **3** colors
- focal bead
- **2** 4mm accent beads
- Nymo D
- beading needles, #12 or Big Eye
- E6000 glue or Terrifically Tacky Tape
- beadweaving loom

[14] Thread a needle on the two center warp threads, and string an accent bead, the focal bead, an accent bead, and an 11º (**photo h**). Skip the 11º and retrace the thread path back to the first accent bead. Remove one thread from the needle and secure the other by weaving into the beadwork. Repeat with the first thread.

[15] Sew down the edges of each section with the remaining warp threads. Trim the tails. ●

LOOMWORK

Twisted bands

Weave a split-loom bracelet with a flair

by **Carol Bauer**

Spice up your loomwork by integrating sections of twisted warps. This bracelet project consists of four regular loomed sections connected by three sections with twisted warps. These directions make a bracelet that is 7¾ in. (19.7cm) long. To make a shorter bracelet, delete an equal number of rows on each end. You will need a loom that can accommodate warp threads at least 18 inches (46cm) long.

[1] Set up your loom with 12 warps (Loomwork Basics, p. 66).
[2] Thread a needle with 4 ft. (1.2m) of the same thread. Leaving a 6-in. (15cm) tail, tie the weft thread to the outer left-hand warp thread (outer right for lefties) at the top of the loom. Following the pattern below, beginning at **point A** and reading each row from top to bottom, string the the 11 beads for the first row. Pass the weft thread under the warp threads.
[3] With your left index finger, push the beads up between the warp threads, with one bead between each pair of threads (**photo a**). Go back through the beads above

A 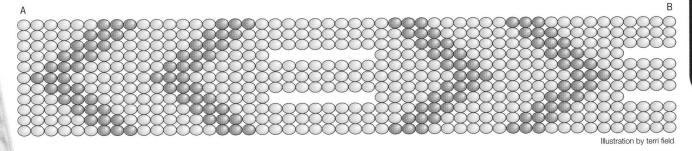 B

Illustration by terri field

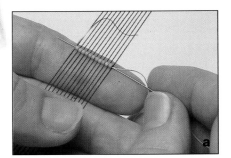
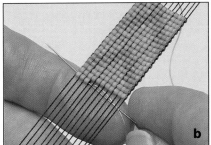
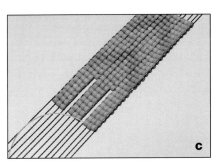

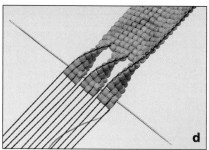

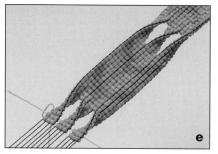

the warp threads from right to left. To make sure you pass over each warp, look for the glint of the needle between the beads.

[4] Weave the next 18 rows, which completes two chevrons.

[5] For row 20, pick up three beads and weave using only the first four warp threads (**photo b**). Continue weaving until you have eight rows of three beads. Zigzag back through the three-bead rows following **figure**. Exit between the fourth and fifth bead of row 19 and weave another three-bead strip. Repeat the split-loom weaving until you have three three-bead strips that are each eight rows long (**photo c**).

[6] Twist the three strips in the same direction with your fingers. Stabilize the twists by inserting a beading needle through the second row from the end (**photo d**).

[7] Pick up 11 beads and weave the first row after the split. If you were originally weaving left to right, you will now be weaving right to left. Be patient, this row can be tricky. After a couple of rows, remove the extra beading needle.

[8] Continue weaving to **point B**, then follow the pattern from **point B** back to **point A**. When you work the next twisted section, twist the strips in the opposite direction from the first section. This will relieve the strain on the warp threads, and it looks nice

MATERIALS
bracelet 7¾ in. (19.7cm)
- Japanese cylinder beads:
  5g color A
  3g color B
- three-strand clasp or 1 or more snap clasps
- 1g size 15º seed beads
- beadweaving loom
- Nymo 0 beading thread
- beading needles, #12
- beeswax

FIGURE

(**photo e**). Finish weaving the pattern, then weave in the weft threads.

[9] Cut the bracelet from the loom, leaving the warps as long as possible.

[10] Determine where your clasp will be attached. Leave two adjacent warp threads for each clasp loop, and weave the rest of the warps into the bracelet. Secure them with half-hitch knots (Basics, p. 5) between beads, and trim. Thread a needle on one remaining warp thread.

[11] Pick up five size 15º seed beads and one clasp loop, then go through the bead between the two warp threads. Retrace the thread path, then tie off the tail in the beadwork with half-hitch knots and trim. Repeat with the other remaining warp thread, but sew through the 15ºs in the other direction. Repeat with any remaining clasps parts.

[12] Alternatively, if your clasps has jump rings, finish off all the warp threads, then simply open a ring (Basics) and slide it through an intersection between the first and second rows. Close the ring. Repeat with any remaining jump rings to attach both halves of the clasp (**photo f**). ●

MORE STITCHES

A tapestry of beads

Square stitch bracelets with vibrant patterns

by **Judy O'Connell**

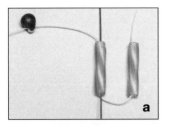

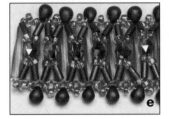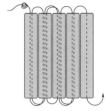

FIGURE 1

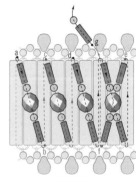

FIGURE 2

FIGURE 3

bugles. Work back through a previous bugle. Tie a second knot on the next thread bridge, then hide the thread in the adjacent bugle, and trim it. Add new thread by reversing this process.

[3] After attaching the final bugle, remove the stop bead. Weave in the tail, tie-off as in step 2, and trim.

Create the picot edging
[1] On the thread that exits the last bugle, pick up three seed beads. Go under the thread bridge between the second and third bugles and back through the last seed bead you added (**photo b**).

[2] Pick up a teardrop and a seed bead. Go under the next thread bridge and through the last seed (**photo c**). Pull it snug. Pick up two seeds. Go under the next thread bridge and through the last seed.

[3] Repeat step 2 until you reach the last bugle (**figure 2**), but do not go under the last thread bridge in the row. This time, go into the bugle and come out the other side. Repeat the picot edging on the opposite side. When you reach the end, go through the bugle and come out the other side.

Top with embellishments
[1] Pick up a small bugle, a seed bead, a crystal, a seed, and a small bugle. Go across the base (**figure 3, a–b**) and through the third bugle in the row (**b–c**). Repeat, but go through every other 12mm bugle (**c–d** and **photo d**). If you are using a different 12mm bugle count, you may not end at the last bugle.

Don't worry—the button will hide the end's imperfections.

[2] Your thread is now exiting from the last—or next to last—12mm bugle. String a small bugle and seed bead. Go through the crystal in the center of the last embellishment. Pick up a seed and small bugle (**e–f**). Go through the bottom of the third 12mm bugle, skipping the middle 12mm bugle as before (**f–g**).

[3] Repeat steps 1 and 2 to complete the row of Xs (**photo e**). Go through the last 12mm bugle.

Finish it off
[1] Pick up an even number of size 11º seed beads to make a loop large enough to go around your button. Here, 26 seed beads were needed for a ⅝-in. (16mm) button.

[2] Go through the opposite end of the bugle, and exit at your starting point, creating a seed bead loop. Work in even count, flat peyote stitch (Basics) for two or three rows

(**photo f**). Tie off the thread with a few half-hitch knots between beads, and trim the thread.

[3] At the bracelet's opposite end, tie on doubled, conditioned thread as before. Pick up four 11ºs, the button's shank, and four 11ºs. Go through the bugle in the opposite direction to complete this loop (**photo g**). Retrace the thread path several times. Tie off the thread with half-hitch knots, and trim the tail. ●

MORE STITCHES

Dresden plate bracelet

Colorful beads highlight a quilter's motif

by **Margaret Scovil**

Seed beads and cube-shaped crystals are perfect partners in this bracelet. The units, reminiscent of quilting's Dresden plate blocks, are stitched individually, then they're sewn together, forming a beautiful band.

Stitching the units

[1] Thread a needle with 1 yd. (.9m) of Nymo. Pick up 12 seed beads and slide them to 6 in. (15cm) from the tail. Go through the beads again to form a circle. Tighten, and tie the tail and working thread together with a square knot (Basics, p. 5). Go through the next four beads (**figure 1, a–b**).
[2] Pick up four seed beads and go back through the same four beads you went through in the same direction as before. Continue through the four beads just added (**b–c**).
[3] Pick up eight seed beads, and go back through the beads you went through in the previous step.

[4] Continue through the next four beads (**c–d**).
[5] Repeat steps 2–4 until you've made a total of ten petals.
[6] Connect the first and last petals by going through the four edge beads of the first petal, the four edge beads of the last petal, and back through the edge beads of the first petal (**e–f**). Your thread will exit toward the center of the circle.
[7] Pick up a bead and go under the thread between the next pair of beads along the inner circle (**figure 2**). Repeat, adding a total of 20 beads around the center. Go through these beads again, keeping the tension snug to tighten the ring.
[8] Work two rows of tubular peyote (Basics) around this ring. Go through both rows of beads again, and tighten the rings (**figure 3**).
[9] Weave through the beads until you reach the ring made in step 7.

Exit at the center of a petal with your needle pointing into the circle. Pick up a crystal, and go through the corresponding bead on the opposite side of the circle (**figure 4**). If you choose a smaller crystal than indicated, pick up a small bead on each side of it to cover any exposed thread.
[10] To fill in the petals, go through a petal bead next to the center circle (**figure 5**, bead 1). Pick up a cylinder bead, go across the petal, and go through bead 2. Pick up two cylinders, go back across the petal, and through bead 3. Pick up three cylinders and go through bead 4.
[11] Repeat step 10 in reverse, working down beads 5–8, as shown in **figure 5**. Continue filling the petals to complete the first Dresden plate unit. Make a total of six units for a small wrist, seven or more for a larger wrist.

FIGURE 1

FIGURE 2

FIGURE 3

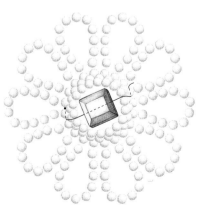

FIGURE 4

Assembling the bracelet

[1] Line up two Dresden plate units so the crystals run horizontally, and note which petal on each unit you'll need to connect. Secure a new thread at the center circle of either of these two petals, and go through the next eight beads (**figure 6, beads 1–8**). Go through the top four beads (**beads 9–12**) of the connecting petal on the second Dresden plate and back through **beads 5–8**. Go through these eight beads several times. Go through **beads 13–16** toward the center of the second plate and through the next four side beads (**beads 17–20**).

[2] Pick up three beads and go through **beads 21–24**, then continue through **beads 1–4**. Pick up three beads and go through **beads 13–16**. Secure the thread in the beadwork with a few half-hitch knots (Basics), trim the thread, and dab the knots with glue.

[3] Repeat steps 1 and 2 to connect the remaining Dresden plate units.

[4] To attach the clasp, secure a new thread in the beadwork at the ring, and weave through the beads until you reach the outer edge of the petal opposite a connecting one. Exit between the center beads. Pick up a seed bead, a 6–7mm bead, and a seed bead. Turn, skip the seed bead, and go back through the large bead and seed bead. Work through the beads, and secure the thread at the center circle (**figure 7**). Knot the thread, trim the ends, and glue the knots.

[5] Start another thread at the other end of the bracelet, and exit the fourth bead on the petal opposite a connecting one (**figure 8, beads 1–4**). Pick up enough seed beads to make a loop that will accommodate the clasp bead, and go back through the petal's top four beads (**beads 8–5**). You can make this loop a single

strand, or work a row or two of peyote stitch to embellish it. Go through the loop as many times as you can for strength. Work back through the petal toward the ring, making several knots along the way. Trim the thread and glue the knots. ●

MATERIALS
bracelet 7 in. (17.5cm)
- 20g seed beads, size 11º, **1 or more** iridescent colors
- 10g Japanese cylinder beads to complement seed beads
- **7 or more** 6mm square crystals
- 6–7mm bead for clasp
- Nymo D
- beeswax or Thread Heaven
- beading needles, #12
- G-S Hypo Cement

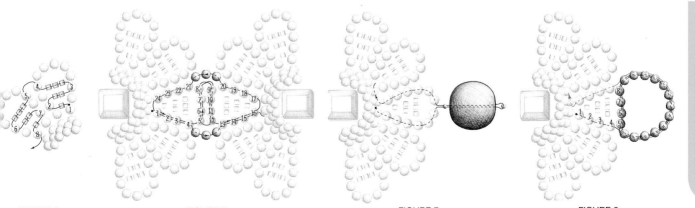

FIGURE 5   FIGURE 6   FIGURE 7   FIGURE 8

MORE STITCHES

Folded and gathered pendant

Have fun with this dimensional free-form technique

by **Beth Stone**

Some say fooling around won't get you far, but, in this case, it's the only way to go. Each of these pendants was made with a unique combination of beads and stitches before being folded and embellished to make a one-of-a-kind accessory.

Think of this pendant as a small bead and stitch sampler—there are no limits to what beads and stitches you can try. Start by making sections for the basic pendant. (You can follow these directions or modify them freely as you work.) Make

each section a different color, and vary the bead sizes and shapes. Then play with the flat piece, folding the sections into layers until you find a version you like. Add pearls, crystals, and other beads to embellish the pendant and to keep the folds in place. Work a few strands of fringe through the bottom edge. The more embellishment you add, the sturdier the pendant becomes.

To string the pendant, run beading wire through a fold or through several well-attached beads, adding

other beads wherever necessary to cover the exposed wire. You can also thread the wire through or around the pendant to suspend other beads below it, as shown in the piece at right. Use the pendants individually or in combination.

Finish stringing your bracelet or necklace with beads that complement the central design. Attach a clasp to the ends of the beading wire with crimp beads (Basics, p. 5).

Section 1

Pick up ten size 11º seed beads on 2 yd. (1.8m) of waxed thread. Work in flat peyote (Basics) for 12 rows (**figure, point 1–2a**).

Section 2

Working in brick stitch (Basics), sew three size 8º beads to the flat (nonworking) edge of section 1 (**figure, point 2a–b**). Work three more rows of brick stitch (**figure, point 2b–c**).

Change direction, and work 11 rows of flat peyote along the non-working brick-stitch edge (17 rows total) (**figure, point 2c–d**). Change direction again and work a four-bead strip of brick stitch along the straight peyote edge for five rows, exiting at **point 3a**.

Section 3

Using a new bead color, pick up four size 8º beads and go through the last "down" 11º in section 1 (**figure, point 3b**). Turn, and pick up an 8º.

Work in flat peyote across the last four beads for 11 rows, exiting at **point 4a**.

Section 4

Pick up 20 size 9º s. Work back in flat peyote and connect this row to two edge beads in section 3 (**figure, point 4b**). Work another row of flat peyote. Turn and work back in two-drop peyote (Basics). Turn and repeat, exiting at **point 5**. This section has a ruffled edge.

Section 5

Pick up six 8º s. Work in flat peyote for a total of 14 rows, exiting at **point 6a**.

Section 6

Working in brick stitch, connect four 11º s to the nonworking edge of section 5. Stitch three more rows (**figure, point 6a–b**). Turn, and work four rows of peyote along the nonworking brick-stitch edge (**figure, point 6b–c**). Turn, and work in brick stitch across the six beads along the edge to **point 7a**.

Section 7

Pick up seven size 8º s (**figure, point 7b**), go through the 8º at the corner of section 5, and pick up another 8º. Work in flat peyote for a total of eight rows, exiting at **point 8**.

Section 8

Pick up six 8º s. Work in flat peyote for a total of ten rows to **point 9a**.

Section 9

Go through the corner bead on the bottom row of section 3. Pick up two cylinder beads (**figure, point 9b**) and go through the next 8º of section 8. Repeat. Turn and work in two-drop peyote for ten rows to **point 10a**.

Section 10

Pick up eight 11º s. Go under the thread bridge between the last two edge beads in section 3 (**figure, point 10b**). Go back through the last bead picked up and work across the row in flat peyote. (Don't use the first bead again.) Turn, and work back across the row. Weave the thread tail into the beadwork and cut. ●

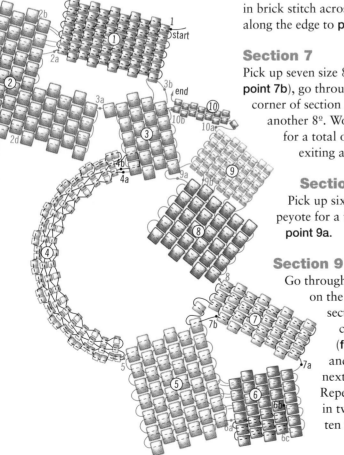

MATERIALS
pendant

- size 8º seed beads in **4** colors, various shapes
- size 9º 3-cuts in **1** color
- size 11º Japanese cylinder beads in **1** color
- size 11º seed beads in **4** colors, various shapes
- assorted pearls, crystals, and beads for embellishment
- Nymo B or D
- beading needles, #10

stringing

- assorted beads to complement pendant
- 2–3 ft. (60–90cm) beading wire, .013 or .014
- **2** crimp beads
- clasp
- chainnose pliers
- crimping pliers

MORE STITCHES

Fringe frenzy

A favorite art bead gets some support

by **Christina Baker**

Large lampwork beads call for a substantial foundation. Here, art beads are showcased between segments of spiral rope embellished with branched fringe. The instructions at right are for the bracelet, but you can easily adapt them to make a matching necklace. Because a necklace can accommodate more weight, feel free to surround your lampwork bead with silver and add more accent beads and drops to the fringe.

Spiral rope

[1] Create a template by cutting a strip of paper the length of your wrist and marking it as shown in **figure 1**.
[2] Begin the spiral rope chain with 1 yd. (.9m) of thread. Pick up four

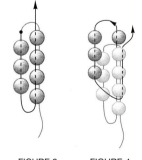

core beads and three outer beads, and slide them down your thread, leaving an 8- to 10-in. (20–25cm) tail (**figure 2**). Go back through the four core beads in the same direction (**figure 3**).

[**3**] Pick up one core bead and three outer beads. Skip the first core bead, and go through the next four core beads (**figure 4**).

[**4**] Adjust the new outer beads to sit against the first group of outer beads (**photo a**).

Using your template as a guide, repeat steps 3 and 4 until you've come to the place for the art bead. Pick up enough core beads to fill the art bead, and string the art bead over them. Resume making the spiral rope (**photo b**). When you reach the length of the template, leave another tail of thread at that end. You'll add additional support for the art bead later.

Adding the clasp

[**1**] At the end of the rope, string one 6mm bead, four seed beads of any color, and the bar end of the clasp. Go back through the four seed beads, the 6mm, and three core beads from the spiral rope.

[**2**] Reverse direction, and retrace the clasp connection several times to make sure it is secure (**photo c**). Work the thread down through the bracelet and tie it off with several half-hitch knots (Basics, p. 5).

[**3**] Add the toggle ring to the other end of the rope the same way, but omit the four seed beads. Retrace the thread path, and end the thread the same way.

Begin the fringe

[**1**] Secure a new 1-yd. (.9m) thread at one end of the spiral rope with half-hitch knots. Exit between the 6mm and the first core bead.

MATERIALS
bracelet 7 in. (17.5cm)
- lampwork bead
- 10g size 11º seed beads in each of **2** colors
- **2** 6mm accent beads
- silver toggle clasp
- Nymo D beading thread
- beading needles, #12

[**2**] Make branched fringe between the core beads as follows: pick up seven seed beads, skip the end bead, and go back through two beads. Pick up three beads. Skip the end bead, and go back through the new beads and the remaining four beads on the main branch. Go through the next core bead, and repeat to make another branched fringe.

[**3**] You may vary the fringe in length, color, and number of branches. To make a three-branched fringe (**photo d**), follow step 2, but instead of going back through all four beads on the main branch, go through two and add another branch of three. Then go back through the remaining two beads on the main branch.

[**4**] Add fringe up to the ¼-in. (6mm) mark on the template preceding the art bead. At this point, shorten fringe so the art bead doesn't get covered.

[**5**] Go through the seed beads and art bead several times to strengthen the connection. You should weave through at least four times. Add branched fringe to the other end of the bracelet. When finished, weave the thread back into the bracelet and tie off with several half-hitch knots. ●

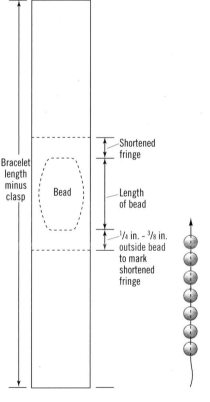

FIGURE 1   FIGURE 2

FIGURE 3   FIGURE 4

Fuchsia trellis bracelet

Transform a daisy chain
into an elegant bracelet

by **Stephanie J. Eddy**

Inspired by the fuchsia—an old-fashioned garden classic—this bracelet is sure to become a favorite. The bracelet's base-row pattern is an offset variation of the daisy chain. Weave additional rows on each side of the base row to complete the fuchsia pattern.

Base row

Keep the tension tight as you work the base row. To maintain the shape and help hold the tension, keep your thumb and forefinger on each new circle of beads as you secure the 3mm bead.

[1] Pick up six color A size 11º seed beads and two color B size 8º seed beads on a 2-yd. (1.8m) length of conditioned Nymo, leaving a 4-in. (10cm) tail. Go through all the beads again to form a circle (photo a).

[2] Position the circle with the working thread at the bottom, and hold the tail with your thumb. Pick up a 3mm bead. Put it in the center of the circle and press it in place. Keeping the tension tight, lay the thread between the fifth and sixth A beads strung (photo b).

[3] Moving clockwise, sew through the next two As (photo c).
[4] Pick up two Bs and five As. Go through the third A of the circle in the same direction as before (photo d) to make another circle (photo e).
[5] Pick up a 3mm bead, press it into the circle, and lay the thread between the third and fourth beads strung.
[6] Moving counterclockwise, sew through the next two As (photo f).
[7] Repeat steps 4–5, then step 3 (photo g, p. 88).
[8] Measure your wrist. Repeat steps 4–7 until the base chain is ¾-in. (1.9cm) shorter than your wrist. End with an even number of circles.

Button

Pick up three As, the button, and three As. Form a loop by going through the three As at the end of the base row (photo h). Reinforce it by retracing the thread path.

Side one

[1] Position the bracelet so the button is at the bottom with the working thread on the right.
[2] Pick up five color C size 15º

seed beads and go through the first B on the base row (photo i).
[3] Pick up one B, one color D size 11º seed bead, and three color E size 15º seed beads. Skip the Es and go through the D again to form a triangle at the tip of the flower. Go through the next B on the base row (photo j).
[4] Pick up five Cs and go through the next base row B.
[5] Repeat steps 3 and 4 to the row's end.
[6] After completing the last flower, do not remove the needle. Tie a surgeon's knot (Basics, p. 5) with the tail and working thread. Dab the knot with glue.

End loop

[1] When the glue is dry, sew through the three As along the left side of the bracelet (photo k).
[2] Pick up 30 As and go back through the three As to form a loop (photo l).
[3] Test the loop to make sure the button passes through it easily. Add or remove beads as needed. Retrace the thread path two or three times.

Side two

[1] Turn the bracelet so the loop is at the bottom with the working thread on the right.

[2] Go through the first B on the base row (**photo m**).

[3] Pick up one D and three As. Skip the Es and go through the D to form the flower tip. Then pick up a B (**photo n**).

[4] Sew through the next B on the base row (**photo o**).

[5] Pick up five Cs. Repeat step 4.

[6] Repeat steps 3–5.

[7] After exiting the last B, retrace the thread path established when adding the button. Tie a surgeon's knot with the tail and working thread and finish off as before. **○**

MATERIALS
bracelet 7½ in. (19cm)
- **28–32** 3mm round fire-polished beads
- seed beads, 5g each:
  size 11º, color A
  size 8º, color B
  size 15º, color C
  size 11º, color D
  size 15º, color E
- ⅝-in. (16mm) diameter button or bead
- Nymo B, black or green
- Thread Heaven
- beading needles, #12
- G-S Hypo Cement

g

h

i

j

k

l

m

n

o

Noughts and crosses bracelet

Stitch a bracelet of geometric components

by **Jane Tyson**

Integrating clasps into beadwoven jewelry so that the clasp becomes a seamless part of the whole piece is a perennial challenge. This bracelet addresses that challenge beautifully with an alternating pattern of diamonds and rings.

For best results, avoid silver-lined bugles as they have narrow holes. Cull the bugle beads so that they are exactly the same length, and discard those with uneven edges. Use Japanese seed beads because they have holes large enough for the multiple thread passes required in this project.

Because 3mm bugles are sometimes difficult to find, this design has been adapted to use 4mm bugles as an alternative. The crosses are slightly larger, and each arm of the cross will require two seed beads rather than one. The black and red bracelet on p. 89 uses 4mm bugles. You must make a larger end ring for the clasp in this version.

Making the cross

[1] Pick up four bugle beads on 2 yd. (1.8m) of thread, leaving a 4-in. (10cm) tail. Tie the working thread and the tail in a square knot (Basics, p. 5), pulling the bugles into a firm square. Sew through the first bugle again (**figure 1**).
[2] Pick up one color A seed bead, and sew through the next bugle. Repeat three times to add an A at each corner of the square. Sew through the next bugle and A in the square (**figure 2**).

[3] Pick up one color B seed bead, an A, and a B (if using 4mm bugles, pick up two Bs, an A, and two Bs). Hold the square so the bead just exited points down, and sew through the left corner bead (**figure 3**). Sew back through the beads added and the seed bead at the bottom corner again. Sew back through the next one (or two) Bs and the center A (**figure 4**).
[4] Pick up one (or two) Bs and sew through the right-corner A, pulling the beads just added into the center of the bugle-bead square. Sew back through the bead(s) just added and the center A so the needle exits in the direction of the top corner bead (**figure 5**).
[5] Pick up one (or two) Bs and sew through the top corner bead, back through the bead(s) just added, through the center A bead, and through the bead(s) added in step 4, exiting the right corner A (**figure 6**).
[6] Turn the cross component over and repeat steps 3–5 to add a cross on the other side.
[7] Pick up three As and sew back through the A just exited. Sew through the four As again to strengthen the connection. Go through two As again to exit the end A (**figure 7**).

Making the nought

[1] Pick up a B, an A, and a B. Go through the A last exited. Continue through a B and an A (**figure 8**). Pick up nine As and go through the A last exited to make a circle of ten As. Continue through one more A in the ten-bead circle (**figure 9**).
[2] To begin adding picots around the circle, pick up a B and an A and sew through the closest B on the connecting loop, the A last exited, and the next A on the circle (**figure 10**).
[3] Repeat step 2 seven times.
[4] Sew through the next B on the connecting loop. Pick up an A, and sew down through the last B in the previous picot to connect the last picot to the first (**figure 11, a–b**).
[5] Go through six As on the central circle to exit at the side of the circle where you will add the next component in the chain (**b–c**).
[6] To start reinforcing the circle, pick up a B and go through the A on the picot connected to the A just exited (**c–d**).
[7] Pick up a B, and sew back through the A last exited on the inner circle and the next A on the inner circle (**d–e**). Tighten so the Bs in the circle's middle line up evenly between the inner and outer A beads.

FIGURE 1

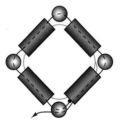

FIGURE 2

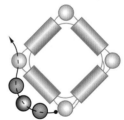

FIGURE 3

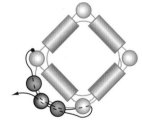

FIGURE 4

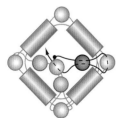

FIGURE 5

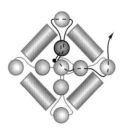

FIGURE 6

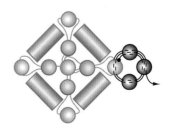

FIGURE 7

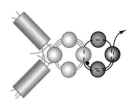

FIGURE 8

FIGURE 9

FIGURE 10

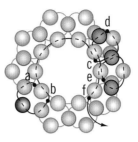

FIGURE 11

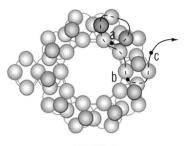

FIGURE 12

[8] Pick up a B. Go through the corresponding A on the picot. Go through the first B added in step 7, the last A exited on the inner circle, and the next A on the inner circle (e–f). Tighten.

[9] Repeat step 8 seven more times, sewing through the previously added B with each repeat.

[10] To finish the reinforcing circle of Bs, sew through the first B on the reinforcing circle, through the corresponding A on the picot, and the last B added. Continue through three As on the inner circle (figure 12, a–b). Go through the next B and the A on the picot (b–c). Make sure you are exiting the picot A opposite from the picot A that is linked to the previous component. There should be four A-bead picots between this A and the linked A on each side of the circle.

[11] Repeat step 7 of "Making the cross."

Completing the bracelet

[1] Alternate crosses and noughts until the chain is long enough to encircle your wrist and ends with a cross. End with step 6 of "Making the cross."

[2] To make the connecting ring for the toggle clasp, you must start with a circle of As large enough for the cross

component to fit through. There are 16 in the bracelet made with 3mm bugle beads and 18 in the one with 4mm bugles. However, test the loop before you begin stitching, as bead sizes vary.

[3] When the size of the ring is correct, end by going through the next A as in step 1 of "Making the nought."

[4] Repeat steps 2–9, amending the number of picot repeats to account for the added beads in the ring. In step 5, sew through only one A on the inner circle because you do not need to end opposite the join to connect another component. Finish reinforcing the circle as in the first part of step 10. Then end the thread in the beadwork with a few half-hitch knots (Basics) before trimming the tail. ●

MATERIALS
bracelet 7½ in. (19cm)

- 3g 3mm Japanese bugle beads or 4g 4mm bugle beads
- Japanese seed beads, size 11º, 5g each of **2** colors
- beading needles, #12
- Nymo D or Silamide
- beeswax or Thread Heaven

MORE STITCHES

Extravagant earrings

Embroidered
components
pair off
in beautiful
earrings

by **Sherry Serafini**

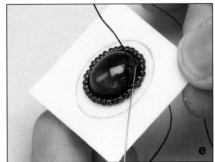

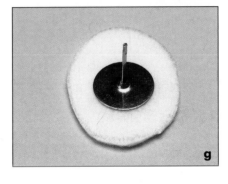

Getting started

[1] Decide on the size and shape of your four components. Determine how much beadwork will surround each cabochon and draw the basic shape with a pencil. Leaving yourself room all the way around, roughly block out and cut each component from the Lacy's Stiff Stuff.

[2] Apply a thin, even layer of E6000 to the back of a cab with a toothpick. Glue one cab in the center of each piece of Lacy's (**photo a**) and let dry.

Beading the bezels

[1] Thread a needle with 1 yd. (.9m) of conditioned Nymo (Basics, p. 5), and knot the end. Come up through the Lacy's against the cab.

[2] Backstitch around the cab using size 14° seed beads, as follows: Pick up three 14°s, and sew back through the fabric right after the last bead. Come up between the second and third bead (**photo b**) and go through the third bead again. Pick up three 14°s (**photo c**) and sew through the fabric of after the last bead (**photo d**). Come up between the second and third bead just added. Repeat around. End with an even number of beads.

[3] Once the cab is encircled, begin even-count circular peyote from the

base row (Basics). Go up through the first bead, pick up one 14°, skip the second bead in the base row, and go through the third bead (**photo e**). Continue around, going through the odd-numbered beads.

[4] If you need to add another row, step up by going through the first beads of rows 1 and 2 (**photo f**).

[5] When the cab is secure, weave through several beads to get back to the Lacy's. Backstitch around the first row of beads. Keep the earring tops simple by backstitching three or four rows around the cab, occasionally stitching in a freshwater pearl on one side.

[6] Repeat steps 1–5 to make the other earring top.

[7] The bottom portions of the earrings are made the same way as the tops, but you can make them more elaborate, if desired. Instead of just circling the cab, stitch in a pearl or a small chunk of stone.

You can also take a second or third row only halfway around your cab to create some interesting shapes.

[8] When all the cabs are beaded, trim the Lacy's. Stay as close to the beadwork as possible, taking care not to cut your threads.

Finishing the backs

[1] For the earring top, apply a thin, even layer of glue to the finding. Place the finding to the Lacy's at the center of the beadwork and let it dry (**photo g**).

[2] Cut out a piece of Ultrasuede the size of your earring top and pierce a tiny hole for the post with a thick needle.

[3] Apply E6000 over the base of the post and the Lacy's.

[4] Place the Ultrasuede over the post, and push the stem through the hole (**photo h**). Smooth it down, and let it dry. Repeat with the other earring top.

[5] Adhere Ultrasuede to the backs of the earring bottoms and let them dry.
[6] Carefully trim the Ultrasuede close to the beadwork.

Finishing the edges
[1] Beading along the edges makes your work look finished and secures the Ultrasuede to the beadwork (**photo i**). Thread 2 yd. (1.8m) of Nymo, and exit through a bead near the edge. Make half-hitch knots (Basics) in between several beads.
[2] Pick up a 14º, and come through an edge bead and through the Ultrasuede.
[3] Come up through the same 14º and pull snug. Continue around until you reach the bead where you started.
[4] Finish by going back through this starting bead, but don't go through the Ultrasuede. Go through a few beads, making half-hitch knots.
[5] Edge all the components.

Connecting tops and bottoms
[1] Locate the center top edge bead of an earring bottom and the center bottom edge bead of an earring top.
[2] Thread a needle with 1½ yd. (1.4m) of Nymo, and weave through the beadwork near the top of an earring bottom. Make a half-hitch knot in between several beads but don't cut the thread.
[3] Go through the center edge bead.

[4] Pick up a 14º, an 8º, and a 14º. Go through the center bottom edge bead of the earring top and pull snug.
[5] Go through this bead again and through the beads just strung. Then go through the edge bead you began with.
[6] Go through the bead next to the connecting bead on the earring bottom and pick up five 14ºs.
[7] Go through the corresponding bead on the earring top and pull snug.
[8] Repeat on the other side of the first group of corresponding beads. You should have a total of three connectors to secure the top of the earring to the bottom (**photo j**). You can also weave through a stone nugget or a large-hole bead to make a secure connection (**photo k**).
[9] Weave through the beadwork towards the bottom of the earring. Don't cut the thread.

Adding fringe
[1] Determine the amount of desired fringe, and weave through to the bottom edge bead where the fringe will start.
[2] Pick up an assortment of beads ending with one 8º, four 14ºs, the bottom fringe bead, and four 14ºs. **Photo l** shows a close up of one of my fringe patterns.
[3] Go back through the 8º and continue through the rest of the fringe beads.

MATERIALS
pair of earrings
- 4 x 4-in. (10 x 10cm) piece of Lacy's Stiff Stuff (505-623-1544, lacysstiffstuff.com)
- 4 x 4-in. piece of Ultrasuede
- 4 cabochons; two matching for the tops and two matching for the bottoms
- assortment of size 14º, 11º, and 8º seed beads, freshwater pearls, Czech faceted rounds, daggers, and drop beads
- pair flatpad ear posts
- Nymo B
- beeswax or Thread Heaven
- beading needles, #12
- E6000 glue

[4] Go through the next bottom edge bead, and repeat steps 2 and 3. One way to vary the fringe length is to add several 14ºs before picking up the rest of the fringe beads. Continue until you've made the desired amount of fringe.
[5] To make a strand to drape across the front of the fringe (**photo m**), go through the next bottom edge bead.
[6] String an assortment of beads, bring the strand across the front of the fringe, and go through the edge bead before the first fringe. Weave back through the beadwork and tie an overhand knot (Basics). Hide the knot, go through a few more beads, and trim the tail. ●

CONTRIBUTORS

Maria Ahasgina lives in Stockholm, Sweden. Contact her via e-mail at maryag@newmail.ru, or visit her Web site, crystaldrops.ru.

Christina Baker has a degree in Fine Arts and creates two-and three-dimensional pieces. She can be reached via e-mail at SJCABaker@aol.com.

Contact Carol Bauer in care of *Bead&Button* or via e-mail at CarolB1234@aol.com.

Perie Brown lives in Canton, Ohio. Contact her at (330) 455-1294, or e-mail her at rkb9@aol.com

Email Yulia Crystal at yulia_crystal@hotmail.com, or visit her Web site www.yuliacrystal.com.

Stephanie Eddy sells kits for her bracelet on her Web site, stephanieeddy.com Call her at (208) 853-7988, or write to her at 7988 W. Arapaho Ct., Garden City, Idaho 83714.

Contact Ann Egan at (610) 262-6507 or e-mail her at annegan@enter.net.

Contact Leslee Frumin at 27332 Silvercreek Dr., San Juan Capistrano, California 92675, or by e-mail leslee@lesleefrumin.com.

Contact Dottie Hoeschen at 3940 Lehnenberg Road, Riegelsville, Pennsylvania 18077, or via e-mail at stonebrash@juno.com.

Carole Horn is a renowned instructor from New York. Reach her at (212) 682-7474, or at carolehorn@nyc.rr.com.

Contact Dina Krieg via e-mail at dinakrieg@hotmail.com.

Laura Jean McCabe can be contacted via e-mail at justletmebead@aol.com.

Contact Sharon McCauley at (414) 354-1530.

Anna Nehs is an associate editor at *Bead&Button* magazine. Contact her at editor@bead&button.com.

Contact Debbie Nishihara in care of *Bead&Button* magazine at editor@bead&button.com.

Contact Judy O'Connell via e-mail at judyoconnell@core.com.

Contact Bonnie O'Donnell-Painter via e-mail at cubuffnut@aol.com.

Contact Glenda Payseno via e-mail at glendapayseno@comcast.net, or write to her at 5906 79th St., Ct. E, Puyallup, Washington 98371-8335.

Don Pierce is the author of *Beading on a Loom* and *Designs for Beading on a Loom*. You can see more of his work at his Web site, donpierce.com.

Maria Rypan has published numerous instruction books and offers kits for projects. Contact her in Canada at (416) 247-1993, or by e-mail at maria@rypandesigns.com.

Contact Nicole Schlinger via e-mail at nicolesl@netins.net, or write to her at 1842 400th Ave., Brooklyn, Iowa 52211.

Contact Margaret Scovil at (503) 694-1320 or mscovilbeads@netscape.net.

Sherry Serafini lives in Natrona Heights, Pennsylvania. Visit her Web site at serafinibeadedjewelry.com.

Beth Stone can be contacted via e-mail at bnshdl@msn.com.

Contact Sylvia Sur via e-mail at ssur@worldnet.att.net.

Jane Tyson lives in Tasmania, Australia, and can be reached via e-mail at lj_tyson@aapt.net.au.

INDEX

Ahasgina, Maria 17
Baker Christina 84
Bauer, Carol 73
bracelets
A tapestry of beads 76
Cabochon connection bracelet 20
Criss-cross embellished bracelet 78
Diamond and arch bracelet 50
Dresden plate bracelet 80
Dynamic cuff 36
Fringe frenzy 84
Fuchsia trellis bracelet 86
Gold-brick bracelet 58
Huichol bracelet 12
Noughts and crosses bracelet 89
Rainforest band 32
Rock garden bracelet 28
Subtle stripes band 24
Twisted bands 73
Woven geometrics 61
brick stitch
Cones of many colors 56
Diamond and arch bracelet 50
Folded and gathered pendant 82
Gold-brick bracelet 58
Starlight, star bright earrings 53
Woven geometrics 61
brooches
Autumn leaves brooch 43
Brown, Perie 24
Crystal, Yulia 20
daisy chain
Fuchsia trellis bracelet 86

earrings
Extravagant earrings 92
Starlight, star bright earrings 53
Eddy, Stephanie J. 86
Egan, Ann 56
embroidery
Extravagant earrings 92
Paisley choker 67
Frumin, Leslee 28
herringbone stitch
Fiery blooms necklace 26
Rainforest band 32
Rock garden bracelet 28
Subtle stripes band 24
Hoeschen, Dorothy 43, 78
Horn, Carole 32
Krieg, Dina 67
ladder stitch
Criss-cross embellished bracelet 78
loomwork
Basics for loomwork 66
Layered loomwork pendant 70
Paisley choker 67
Twisted bands 73
McCabe, Laura Jean 46
McCauley, Sharon 53
Nehs, Anna 50
necklaces
Circuitry collar 46
Cones of many colors 56
Fiery blooms necklace 26
Floating rings necklace 41
Fringe frenzy 84
Netted pendant 17
Paisley choker 67
Ukrainian netted necklace 14
Woven geometrics 61

netting
Cabochon connection bracelet 20
Huichol bracelet 12
Netted pendant 17
Ukrainian netted necklace 14
Nishihara, Debbie 26
O'Connell, Judy 76
O'Donnell-Painter, Bonnie 41
Payseno, Glenda 58
pendants
Folded and gathered pendant 82
Layered loomwork pendant 70
Netted pendant 17
peyote stitch
Autumn leaves brooch 43
Circuitry collar 46
Dynamic cuff 36
Floating rings necklace 41
Folded and gathered pendant 82
Woven geometrics 61
Pierce, Don 70
Rypan, Maria M. 14
Schlinger, Nicole 61
Scovil, Margaret 80
Serafini, Sherry 92
spiral rope
Fringe frenzy 84
square stitch
A tapestry of beads 76
Stone, Beth 82
Sur, Sylvia 12, 36
Tyson, Jane 89